U.S. Navy Floatpl

of World War II

in Action

By Al Adcock

Color by Don Greer

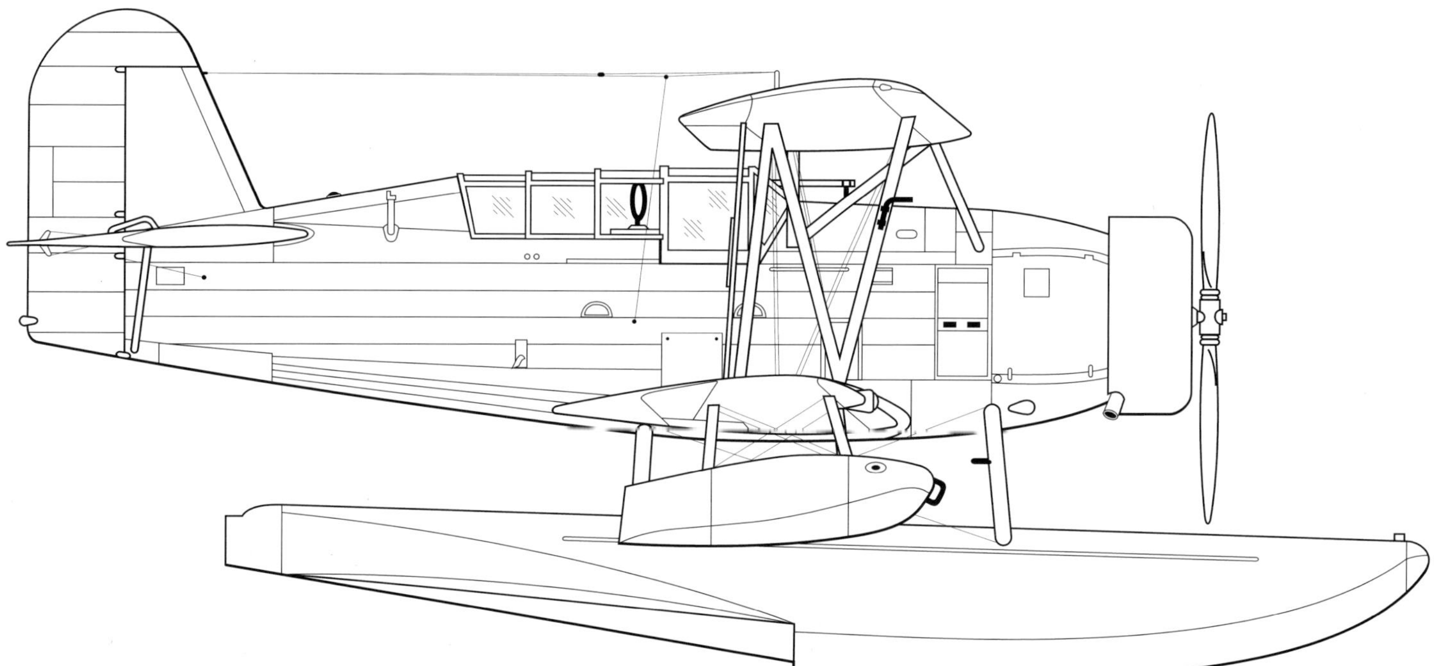

Squadron/Signal Publications

Aircraft Number 203

Cover: A Curtiss SOC-3 Seagull spots gunfire for USS *Augusta* (CA-31) as the cruiser shells the coast of Morocco near Casablanca in support of Operation Torch, the allied invasion of North Africa, in November 1942.

ISBN 0-89747-506-2

If you have any photographs of aircraft, armor, soldiers or ships of any nation, particularly wartime snapshots, why not share them with us and help make Squadron/Signal's books all the more interesting and complete in the future? Any photograph sent to us will be copied and the original returned. The donor will be fully credited for any photos used. Please send them to:

Squadron/Signal Publications, Inc.
1115 Crowley Drive
Carrollton, TX 75011-5010

Если у вас есть фотографии самолётов, вооружения, солдат или кораблей любой страны, особенно, снимки времён войны, поделитесь с нами и помогите сделать новые книги издательства Эскадрон/Сигнал ещё интереснее. Мы переснимем ваши фотографии и вернём оригиналы. Имена приславших снимки будут сопровождать все опубликованные фотографии. Пожалуйста, присылайте фотографии по адресу:

Squadron/Signal Publications, Inc.
1115 Crowley Drive
Carrollton, TX 75011-5010

軍用機、装甲車両、兵士、軍艦などの写真を所持しておられる方はいらっしゃいませんか？どの国のものでも結構です。作戦中に撮影されたものが特に良いのです。Squadron/Signal社の出版する刊行物において、このような写真は内容を一層充実し、興味深くすることができます。当方にお送り頂いた写真は、複写の後お返しいたします。出版物中に写真を使用した場合は、必ず提供者のお名前を明記させて頂きます。お写真は下記にご送付ください。

Squadron/Signal Publications, Inc.
1115 Crowley Drive
Carrollton, TX 75011-5010

Acknowledgements

EDO
United Technologies
Real War Photos
Floating Drydock
U.S. Navy
LTV
Naval Historical Center
National Archives
Elsilrac
Fred C. Dickey Jr.
U.S. Coast Guard
The Tailhook Association
Commander Doug Siegfried USN (Ret.)
William T. Larkins
Peter M. Bowers

Author's Note

This title covers the four major scout floatplanes that were deployed aboard U.S. Navy cruisers, battleships, and, in some small measure, destroyers during World War II. The four aircraft types enjoyed, for the most part, good fortunes and played an important role in spotting for gunfire, liaison, search and rescue, and, of course, observation and scouting.

‣ 'Black 13,' a Vought-Sikorsky OS2U-3 (BuNo 5865) from an inshore scouting squadron, flies out over the Atlantic coast in early 1942. The Kingfisher is camouflaged in nonspecular Blue Gray upper surfaces over nonspecular Light Gray with nonspecular Insignia Red and nonspecular White tail stripes. The gunner/observer has his .30-caliber machine gun deployed and ready for action. (National Archives)

13
13

Introduction

Before the advent of radar and other electronic devices aboard warships, the jobs of seeking out the enemy and spotting of naval gunfire fell to the floatplane scouts. These small one- and two-seat catapult-launched aircraft served aboard U.S. Navy ships as the eyes of the fleet until mid-1949.

The father of the U.S. Navy floatplane is generally considered to be Glenn L. Curtiss, who was the first aviator to fly an aircraft off a ship and the first to land on a ship. In January 1911 he became the first American to land a floatplane, one of his own design, on water (a Frenchman had performed the same feat a year earlier). Aircraft designed by the Curtiss Aircraft Company flew off U.S. Navy ships from 1911 to 1949. Other notable early designers of aircraft for the U.S. Navy were Donald Douglas and Chance Vought.

The introduction of the ship-borne aircraft catapult was an important step forward in naval aviation. The first catapult launch of an aircraft from a U.S. ship occurred 12 July 1916, when the armored cruiser *North Carolina* launched an AB-3 trainer from a fixed, stern-mounted catapult. By the time the U.S. entered World War I, the cruiser *Huntington* had been fitted with a catapult. However, a fixed catapult required the ship to turn into the wind to launch the aircraft and to come to a standstill to recover the plane. During peacetime these were not issues, but wartime conditions posed vastly different problems. The development of the recovery sled, a simple cargo net streamed in the water from the ship, enabled aircraft recovery while the ship was underway, and the adoption of rotating catapults allowed aircraft to be launched into favorable winds regardless of the ship's direction of movement.

Scout floatplanes served in battleships (BB), light cruisers (CL), heavy cruisers (CA), and six *Fletcher*-class destroyers (DD) during World War II. Most battleships carried up to four aircraft, while cruisers with aircraft hangars could accommodate up to eight aircraft, some unassembled. Destroyers were limited to one aircraft, because there were no facilities to store more. Scout planes were not very popular aboard ship; aircraft required storage of highly flammable aviation gasoline, and the aircraft crew and maintenance personnel had to be berthed. All took up valuable space.

Aircraft assigned to ships were organized into Observation Squadrons, designated as 'VO' ('V' for heavier-than-air and 'O' for observation), or Scouting Squadrons, designated 'VCS,' The VOs served on battleships, and VCSs ('C' for cruiser and 'S' for scouting) served in the cruisers. The primary duty of the planes assigned to battleships was to spot for gunfire, while the cruisers' aircraft scouted for the enemy.

There were four types of scout aircraft that served aboard cruisers and battleships during World War II, and three of these were designed by Curtiss. The Curtiss SOC/SON Seagull was the only biplane to serve aboard ship during the war. It was to have been replaced by the Curtiss SO3C Seamew, but the Seamew proved to be ineffective as a scouting aircraft and served mainly as a land-based trainer. Vought's OS2U/OS2N Kingfisher was the only offering not built by Curtiss to serve in the observation and scouting roles during the conflict in the Atlantic and Pacific. The Navy's need for a scout floatplane possessing a higher speed and increased range led to the single-seat Curtiss SC Seahawk, which served from 1944 until early 1949.

Three manufacturers built these floatplanes. The Curtiss-Wright Corporation produced the SOC, SO3C, and the SC; Chance Vought (Vought-Sikorsky), a division of United Technologies, produced the OS2U; while the Naval Aircraft Factory, which by law could construct up to ten percent of the navy's aircraft, produced both the SON and the OS2N. (Under the Navy's aircraft designator system, Curtiss was assigned the letter 'C,' Vought the letter 'U,' and the Naval Aircraft Factory — NAF — the letter 'N.')

All of these floatplanes carried both offensive and defensive armament. The two-seat planes were fitted with .30-caliber (7.62 mm) machine guns, a single weapon each for both pilot and

▼ A VE-7 (Bureau of Aeronautics serial number—'BuNo'—A5970) built by the Naval Aircraft Factory (NAF) is catapulted from the battleship USS *Maryland* (BB-46) in 1933. The VE-7 was a tandem two-seat advanced trainer designed by Lewis-Vought and adapted to catapult use by removing the landing gear and adding floats. (Real War Photos)

▼ This Vought O3U-3 (BuNo 9142), was the first of seventy-six built for the U.S. Navy in 1934. Construction was of doped fabric over a metal frame, and the engine was a 550-horsepower Pratt & Whitney R1340-12 radial. Fabric surfaces are painted aluminum, and metal panels are painted Light Gray. Top surface of the upper wing is Orange Yellow. (LTV)

observer. A few of the SO3Cs were equipped with a .50-caliber (12.7 mm) machine gun for the observer. Each gun was provided with six hundred rounds. The single-seat SC was fitted with a single .50-caliber (12.7 mm) machine gun in each wing. All of the aircraft could be fitted with bomb racks accommodating hundred-pound (45.36 kg) or 250-pound (113.4 kg) bombs or 325-pound (147.42 kg) depth charges.

A few floatplanes had rudimentary radar. Two Curtiss SO3C-1s (BuNos 4804 and 4861) that served on the light cruiser USS *Denver* (CL-58) in late 1942 and early 1943 were fitted with Air-to-Surface Type B (ASB) radar and Yagi antennas on their lower wings. Curtiss SC-1s and SC-2s could be fitted with an AN/APS-4 radar pod under the starboard wing. A lack of sufficient generator power in the Seagull and Kingfisher precluded the installation of any electronic equipment but radio.

Most of the floatplanes could be fitted with landing gear for operation from land, once the floats were removed. Beaching gear could also be attached to the centerline float so the aircraft could be recovered ashore. Removal of floats and installation of auxiliary landing gear usually resulted in an increase in top speed of up to 40 mph (64.3 km/hr), as drag was greatly reduced.

During World War II, U.S. allies were provided with the OS2U Kingfisher and SO3C Seamew under various Lend-Lease agreements. The British found the Kingfishers very useful and placed them in squadron service aboard ship and in the training role until 1944, when they became surplus with the Royal Navy's abandonment of shipboard catapult aircraft. Kingfishers also served with the Royal Australian Navy and the armed forces of Mexico, Chile, Russia (where they served aboard the U.S. cruiser *Milwaukee*, which was temporarily transferred to the Soviet Navy and renamed *Murmansk* by the Soviets), Uruguay, Argentina, and the Netherlands East Indies (NEI). The NEI aircraft were sent to Australia when the Japanese invaded in 1941. The Royal Navy tested the Seamew in 1942 but found it to be completely inadequate for shipboard service, a finding also reached by the U.S. Navy. Seamews were also supplied to the Cuban Air Force.

Camouflage and Markings

Early U.S. Navy shipboard aircraft were painted in an overall finish of aluminum fabric surfaces and Light Gray metal surfaces, with the top of the wing painted Orange Yellow (also called Chrome Yellow) for increased visibility in case of a forced water landing. The U.S. national insignia appeared in four postions on the top and bottom surfaces of both port and starboard wings. Tails and cowlings were painted in various squadron and section colors. In 1940, the U.S. national insignia was added to the forward fuselages of aircraft operating in the Atlantic as part of the Neutrality Patrol. With the beginning of war in Europe and storm clouds developing in Asia, the bright colors were abandoned for an overall nonspecular (flat) Light Gray finish in early 1941. August 1941 saw yet another change, when upper surfaces were ordered painted nonspecular Blue Gray and lower surfaces nonspecular Light Gray, with rudders striped in Insignia Red and Insignia White. This scheme was utilized until January 1943, when a three-color scheme was adopted. Semi-gloss Sea Blue was to be applied to upper surfaces, and nonspecular Insignia White to the lower surfaces. The sides of the aircraft and leading edges of the wings and other flying surfaces were to be painted Intermediate Blue. The final change during World War II took place in June of 1944, when the Bureau of Aeronautics directed that shipboard aircraft were to be painted overall gloss Sea Blue. Changes were sometimes slow to be implemented due to wartime conditions, and there was, understandably, some overlap. For a more in-depth explanation of U.S. Navy camouflage, see *U.S. Navy Aircraft Camouflage & Markings 1940-1945* by Thomas E. Doll, from Squadron/Signal Publications. (▸▸ 7)

▲ Vought's XO5U-1 (BuNo 9399) was designed to the same specifications as the Douglas XO2D-1 and the winning Curtiss XO3C-1, the aircraft that would become the SOC-1 Seagull. All three prototypes were fitted with amphibious gear so they could operate from land or water without use of beaching gear. Of note are the overwing spoilers, the arresting gear for carrier operations, and a canopy for only the pilot. (LTV)

▼ Vought's XSO2U-1 (BuNo 1440) was designed to the same specifications as the Curtiss XSO3C-1, which called for a floatplane that could be reconfigured as a land plane, powered by the 550-horsepower Ranger XV-770-4 inline air-cooled engine. The XSO3C-1 was declared the winner and went into production as the SO3C-1 Seamew. (National Archives)

Development

XO3C-1

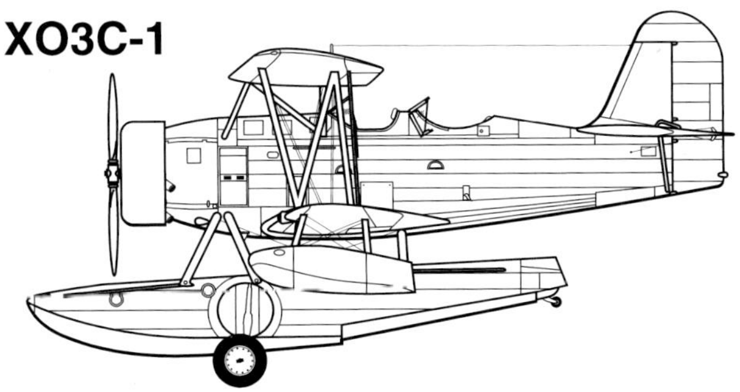

SOC

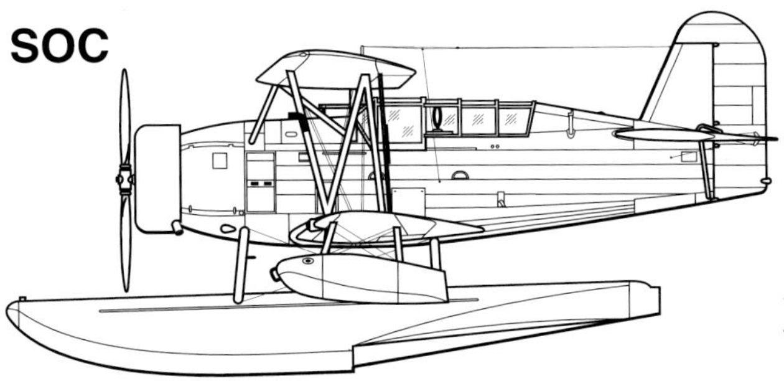

SOC-3A

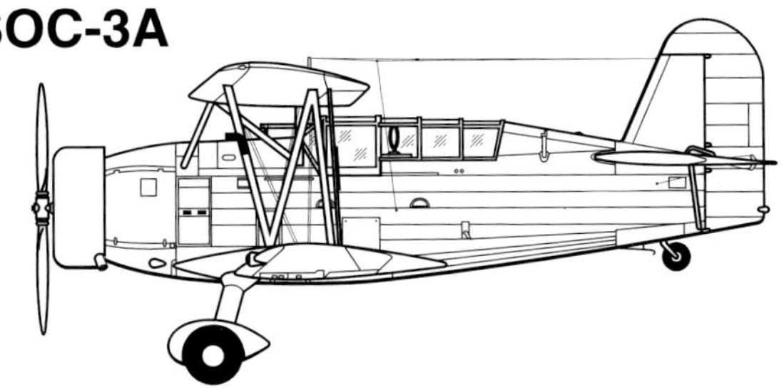

XOS2U-1

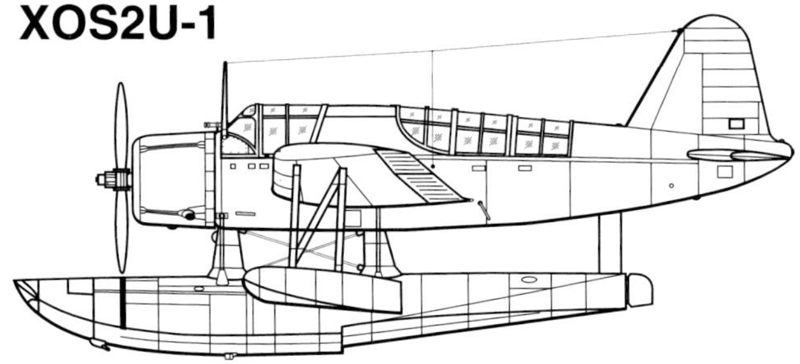

OS2U-3

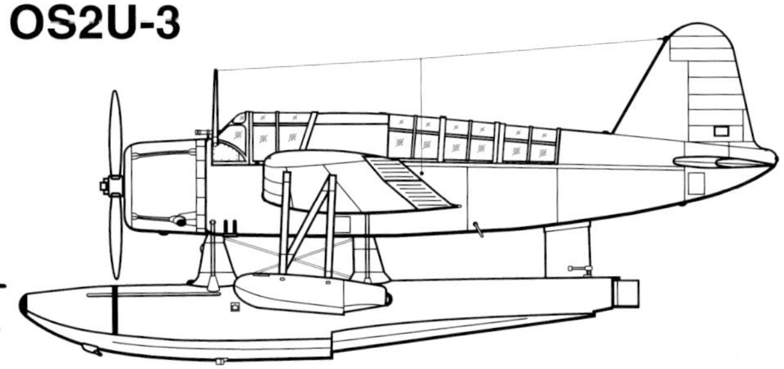

XSO2U-1

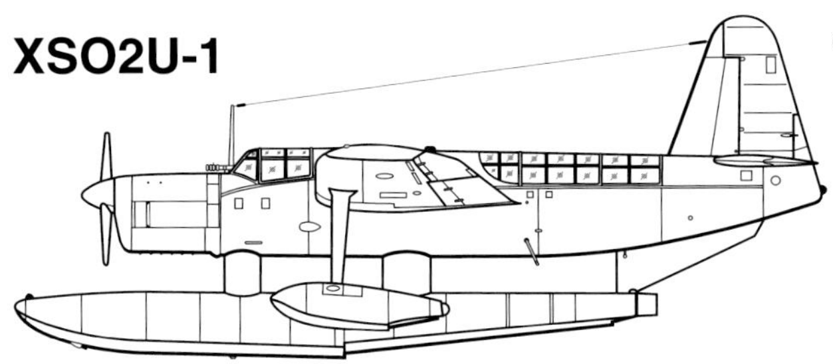

XSO3C

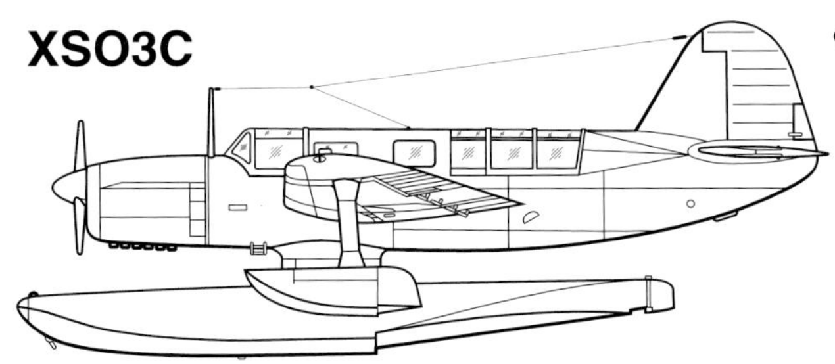

SO3C-1

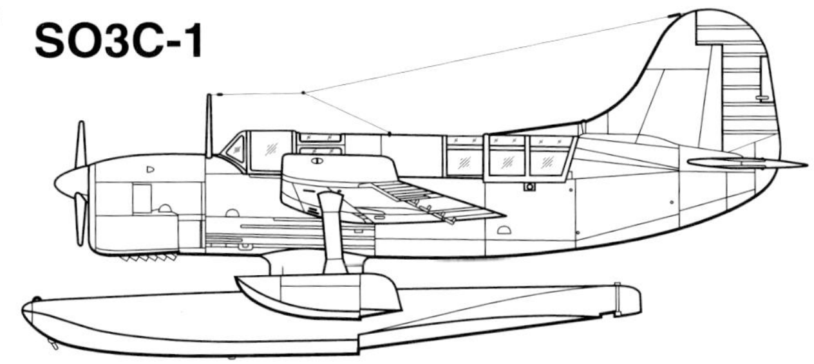

SC-1

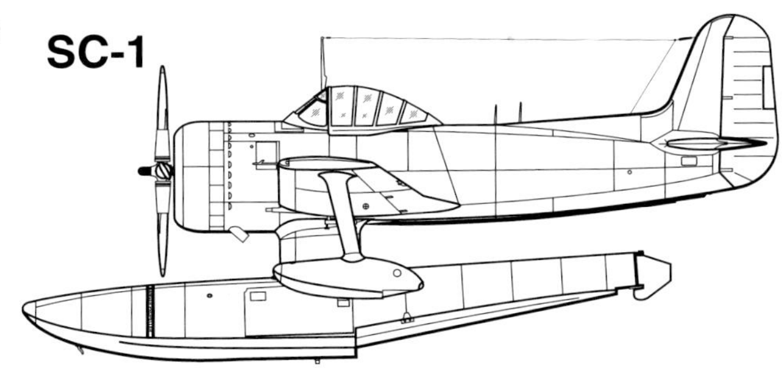

SC-2

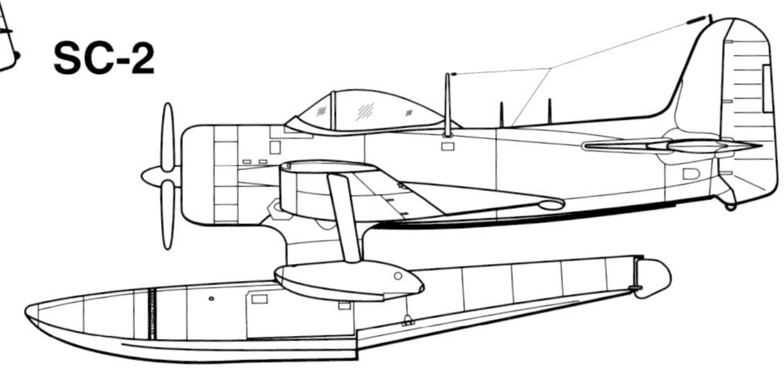

Curtiss SOC Seagull

The Curtiss SOC Seagull was the only U.S. Navy float biplane to serve aboard ship during World War II. The prototype XO3C-1 (BuNo 9413), which first flew on 5 March 1934, was an amphibian equipped with retractable landing gear on the center float and was the winner of a competition for a floatplane to replace Vought and Berliner-Joyce aircraft. Douglas's XO2D-1 and Vought's XO5U also competed for the Navy contract.

The XO3C-1 was powered by a Pratt & Whitney R-1340-12 Wasp radial engine producing 550 horsepower. The crew of two—pilot and gunner/radio operator/observer—sat in open cockpits, protected only by windshields. Wingspan was 36 feet (11.58 m), length was 30 feet 3 inches (9.30 m), and height was 15 feet 7 inches (4.60 m). Empty weight was 3,582 pounds (1,624.8 kg), gross weight 5,236 pounds (2,375 kg). Top speed was 150 mph (241.4 km/hr), and cruising speed was 100 mph (160.9 km/hr). Range with internal fuel of 140 gallons (530 l) was 770 miles (1,239 km).

Following trials and acceptance, the Navy issued a contract for 135 SOC-1s (BuNos 9856–9990), and deliveries began in November 1935. The production SOC-1 was essentially the same as the prototype, with the exception of a change to a Pratt & Whitney R-1340-18 Wasp radial engine and a reduction in height to 14 feet 10 inches (4.52 m) due to removal of the float-mounted landing gear to save weight. The airframe was of aluminum (wings) and welded steel tubing (fuselage) covered with fabric. A single fixed .30-caliber machine gun was provided for the pilot and a flexible .30-caliber machine gun for the observer. Production aircraft also featured a full canopy for the crew, and the 'turtle deck' between the gunner's cockpit and the vertical stabilizer could be lowered to provide for greater movement for the observer's gun. The upper wing featured Handley-Page automatic slats that improved performance at slow speeds and high angles of attack. Underwing bomb racks could accept hundred-pound (45.4 kg) or 250-pound (113.4 kg) bombs or depth charges of 325 pounds (147.4 kg), but with a corresponding reduction in fuel and an increase in drag.

The first SOC-1 went into service on 12 November 1935 aboard the light cruiser USS *Marblehead* (CL-12), replacing the Berliner-Joyce OJ-2. A few SOC-1s were converted to SOC-3A standards with the addition of arresting and catapult gear.

In October 1936 the Navy ordered forty land-based versions of the SOC-1, designated SOC-2 (BuNos 0386–0425). A few SOC-2s were fitted with arresting gear and designated as SOC-2A; these aircraft served with Scouting and Escort Scouting Squadrons aboard escort carriers as trainers and 'hacks.' The SOC-2A also could be fitted with an under-fuselage rack accommodating a 325-pound depth charge or a 500-pound (228.6 kg) bomb.

The final production model of the SOC, the SOC-3, had interchangeable wheel/float gear. A total of eighty-three were built (BuNos 1064–1146), with two (BuNos 1126 and 1127) going to the U.S. Marines Corps, where they served with Marine Scouting Squadron Two (VMS-2). The U.S. Coast Guard acquired the last three SOC-3s produced, designating them SOC-4 and giving them serial numbers V-171 through V-173. They were returned to the U.S. Navy in 1942 as BuNos 48243 through 48245 respectively, after conversion back to SOC-3A standards.

In January 1937, the only Curtiss XSO2C-1 (BuNo 0950) was first flown. Built for evaluation against the Vought-Sikorsky XOS2U-1, this was an SOC-3 with a five-foot extension to the fuselage and flaps on both upper and lower wings, and powered by a R-1340-36 Wasp radial engine of six hundred horsepower. The XSO2C-1's advantages were not deemed significant, and the Navy elected to order more SOCs as well as the OS2U-1.

Curtiss built a total of 271 SOCs in all models at Buffalo, New York, and the Naval Aircraft Factory in Philadelphia, Pennsylvania, built forty-four SOC-3s, designated SON-1 (Bureau Numbers 1147–1190). SON-1s converted for carrier operations with the addition of arresting gear were redesignated SON-1A.

In 1941, just before the U.S. officially entered World War II, all SOC models were given the name 'Seagull.' Considered obsolete at the beginning of the war, the Seagull was destined to be replaced by the Curtiss SO3C Seamew. However, when sea trials and operational tests of the Seamew found it to be inadequate, the SOC was retained by the Navy. Replacing its intended replacement, Curtiss's Seagull continued to serve until victory was achieved in 1945. (⏩ 21)

▲ **The prototype XSOC-1 (BuNo 9413) was originally designated XO3C-1 and had amphibious landing gear and open cockpits. It crashed at Naval Air Station (NAS) Jacksonville in June 1941 and served as a ground instructional airframe until the end of World War II. (National Archives)**

▼ **The prototype XSOC-1 on the after deck of the destroyer *Noa* (DD-343) for tests. The XSOC-1 was assigned to Cruiser Scouting Squadron Three (VCS-3) and given the aircraft number '4.' Following the tests, which began 10 April 1940 and concluded in June, the Navy decided to modify six *Fletcher*-class destroyers to carry a single floatplane, although the aircraft selected to serve aboard was the Vought OS2U. (Floating Drydock)**

◂ The first production SOC-1 (BuNo 9856) sits on the ramp at Anacostia, Maryland, in 1935, painted overall in aluminum dope with Orange Yellow wing tops. The aircraft was constructed of doped fabric over a steel and aluminum airframe, with skin panels of aluminum in high-stress areas. The first SOC-1 was unarmed, but later aircraft had a pair of .30-caliber machine guns. (The Tailhook Association)

▾ An SOC-1, aircraft number three ('4-O-3') from VO-4, prepares to launch cross-deck off the fantail mounted catapult on the battleship USS *West Virginia* (BB-48) in 1938. The aircraft handling crane has been positioned so as not to interfere with the launch. The aircraft is overall aluminum, and the top of the upper wing is Orange Yellow. The tail is Black, and the lower half of the cowling is Red. (Via Tailhook Association)

▾ An SOC-1, aircraft number one ('4-O-1') from Battleship Observation Squadron Four (VO-4), prepares to launch off of the number three turret-mounted catapult of *West Virginia* in 1938. The tail is painted Black, fuselage stripe and cowl are painted Red, and the squadron emblem is painted on the fuselage below the cabane struts. *West Virginia* was the Flagship of Battle Force, Battleships, San Pedro, California. (Via Tailhook Association)

Seagulls of Cruiser Scouting Squadron Five (VCS-5) sit ready on the catapults of USS *Salt Lake City* (CA-25), as the heavy cruiser fires her 8-inch (203 mm) guns at Wake Island on 24 February 1942. The raid was one of the first strikes against the Japanese after Pearl Harbor. National insignias still carry the red center disc. (Real War Photos)

An SOC taxis in San Francisco Bay off Alameda, California, in 1942. The leading edge slats and the upper wing flaps are deployed for takeoff. Bomb racks are fitted to the wings. The SOC was used for training and as squadron hacks, as well as spotting for gunfire and scouting for the enemy. The national insignia is painted oversize on the fuselage side. (National Archives)

Three SOCs from an unidentified Cruiser Scouting Squadron fly over the Pacific Ocean in 1944. The aircraft are armed with a single 250-pound bomb under each wing, indicating they are on anti-submarine patrol. The aircraft are in friendly airspace, as the gunners do not have the 'turtle decks' lowered for gun deployment. (Real War Photos)

Curtiss SOC/SON

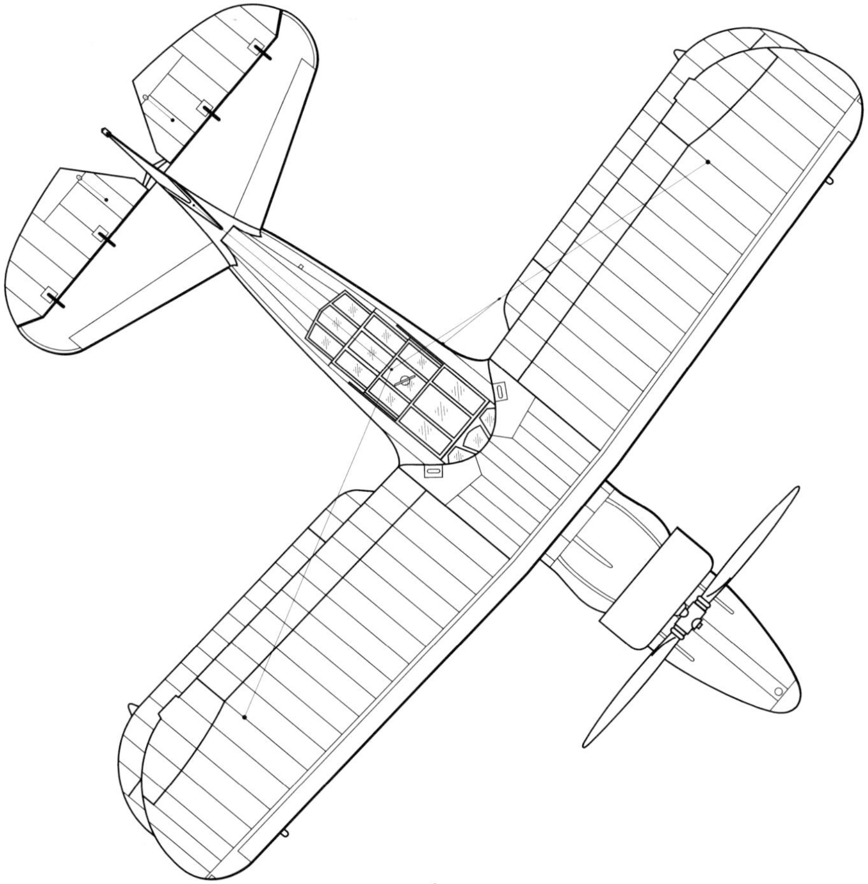

Specifications (SOC-3)

Length .... 32 ft 3 in (9.83 m)
Wingspan .... 36 ft (10.97 m)
Height .... 14 ft 10 in (4.52 m)
Weight, empty ... 3,648 lb (1,654.7 kg)
Weight, maximum . 5,302 lb (2,405 kg)
Engine .... One 550 hp Pratt & Whitney R-1340-18 Wasp aircooled 9-cylinder radial engine
Maximum speed . . 162 mph (260.7 km/h)
Cruising speed . . . 125 mph (201 km/hr)
Fuel .... 170 gal (643.5 l)
Range .... 878 mi (1,413 km)
Rate of climb .... 847 ft/min (4.3 m/sec)
Service ceiling ... 15,800 ft (4,816 m)
Armament .... One fixed forward-firing .30-caliber (7.62 mm) machine gun
One aft-firing .30-caliber (7.62 mm) machine gun on flexible mount
Crew 2

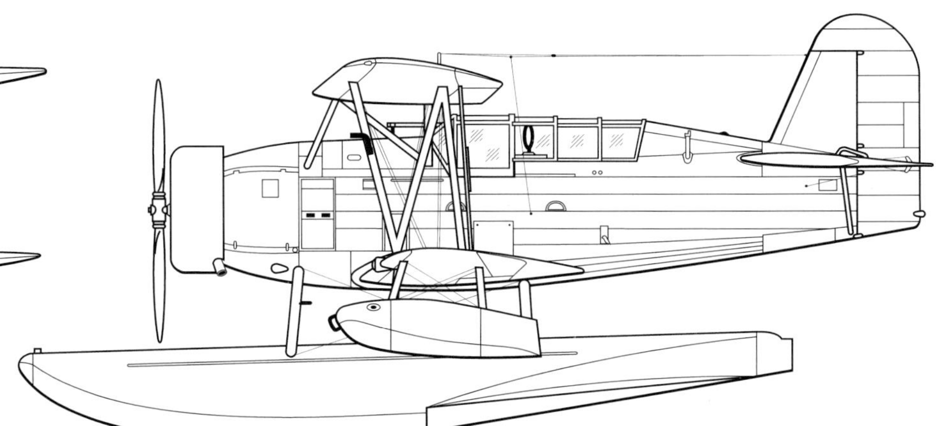

▲ An SOC-1 from Cruiser Scouting Squadron Seven (VCS-7) has caught the sled streamed out by the recovery crew of the heavy cruiser USS *Tuscaloosa* (CA-37) operating in the Atlantic in July 1943. The SOC carries the side marking '7-CS-6,' indicating it is the sixth aircraft assigned to VSC-7. The observer/gunner has climbed out over the canopy and awaits the arrival of the recovery cable. (Real War Photos)

▸ The crew of this SOC, pilot Ensign W.C. Orr and Aviation Radioman 3/c Thomas D. Everett, examine the hole in the left wing caused by Japanese anti-aircraft artillery fire while they were spotting for gunfire over Palau on 26 February 1945. The aluminum wing spars and doped fabric covering of the Seagull stood little chance from enemy gunfire. Aircraft with this kind of damage were repaired using complete wings carried as spares by the ship's aviation department. (Real War Photos)

▾ The observer/gunner of this SOC-1 from VCS-7 has secured the recovery cable to the top wing, and the aircraft is being brought aboard to be placed onto the waiting catapult of *Tuscaloosa* during operations in the Atlantic in July 1943. The SOC-1 is camouflaged in nonspecular Blue Gray over nonspecular Light Gray with the national insignia in four positions. (Real War Photos)

▲ The aviation radioman of this SOC-2 signals with his right hand that he has radio problems while spotting for gunfire for the heavy cruiser USS *Augusta* during Operation Torch, the invasion of North Africa, on 8 November 1942. 'Black 18,' from Cruiser Scouting Squadron Seven (VCS-7), is camouflaged in nonspecular Blue Gray over nonspecular Light Gray, while the national insignia has a Yellow surround. Wing flaps and slats are deployed for slow speed flight. (Real War Photos)

▼ An SOC-2 from VCS-6 is brought aboard the heavy cruiser USS *Minneapolis* (CA36) following a gunfire spotting mission during a raid on Wake Island on 5 October 1943. The U.S. national insignia has been painted oversize, and the camouflage paint shows signs of wear. (Real War Photos)

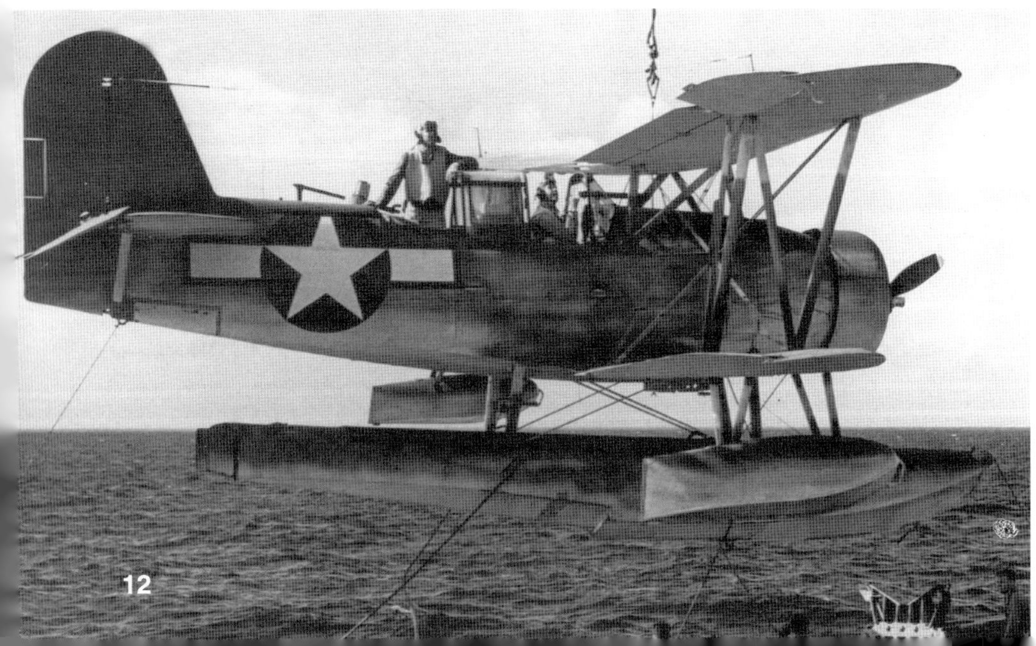

▲ Three SOC-1s and one SOC-2, all from Cruiser Scouting Squadron Six (VCS-6), sit secured with folded wings on the port and starboard catapults on the heavy cruiser USS *Quincy* (CA-39) while she undergoes repairs and refitting at New York Navy Yard on 29 May 1942. The Seagulls are camouflaged in nonspecular Blue Gray over nonspecular Light Gray, with the national insignia applied in six positions. *Quincy* was sunk on 9 August 1942 while operating off of Savo Island. (Real War Photos)

▼ An SOC-2 (BuNo 0403) from VCS-6 on a flight off *Minneapolis*, flagship of Cruiser Division Six. The SOC is painted overall aluminum with Orange Yellow upper wing top surfaces. Tail stripes are Black. The automatic Handley Page wing slats are deployed, indicating the aircraft is approaching stall speed (65 mph).

▲ An SOC-2A makes an arrested landing on the escort carrier USS *Copahee* (CVE-12) on 24 August 1942 while the ship rides at anchor, the first landing by an SOC on the small 'Jeep' carrier. The leading edge automatic slats and flaps are deployed for the tail wheel-first landing. The SOC is camouflaged in nonspecular Blue Gray over nonspecular Light Gray, with the U.S. national insignia in six positions. (Real War Photos)

▼ The wings of SOCs could be folded for stowage aboard battleships and cruisers, as demonstrated by this SOC-1 (BuNo 9908) of VCS-6 on wheels. Tail stripes are Black, and cowling and fuselage band are White. (Peter M. Bowers)

Underwing Ordnance

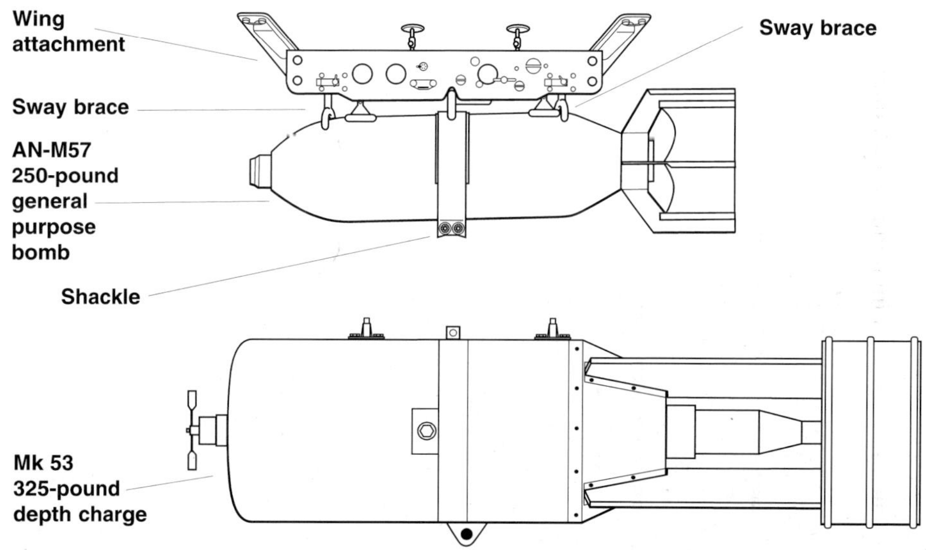

▲ A pair of SOC-3 Seagulls are positioned on the fantail catapults of the light cruiser USS *Boise* (CL-47) in July 1942 as she prepares to raid Japanese-held waters. The aircrew are conferring on the hangar deck cover, and the landing mats are positioned for deployment off the side. The aircraft will be catapulted cross deck, which was a common practice for cruisers with catapults mounted on the fantail. (U.S. Navy)

▼ The Admiral's 'barge,' an SOC-3 (BuNo 1079), sits in the lagoon of the Oakland, California, airport in June 1939. The 'Flagplane' is painted overall Admiral Blue with the main float and wing floats in aluminum. The SOC was the personal mount of Admiral Claude C. Bloch, Commander-in-Chief of the U.S. Fleet (CinCUS), and was based aboard his Flagship, the battleship USS *Pennsylvania* (BB38). (Wm. T. Larkins)

▼ An SOC-3 from VCS-7 taxis up to catch the recovery mat prior to being hoisted aboard the heavy cruiser USS *Tuscaloosa*, operating in the Atlantic during August 1943. The SOC has landed in the slick created when the cruiser made a turn to port, creating a smooth surface for the floatplane's landing. The recovery crew awaits the aircraft's arrival and will place it on the port side catapult. (Real War Photos)

▾ A SOC-3 from VCS-6 catapults off the heavy cruiser USS *Augusta*, operating in the Atlantic in June 1942, for anti-submarine patrol. The SOC has a Red and White striped rudder and is carrying hundred-pound bombs under each wing. The position of the elevators indicates the pilot has the stick pulled back. When the aircraft reaches the end of the catapult, its speed will be 70 mph, sufficient for flight. (Real War Photo)

▴ A SOC-3 from VCS-5 is launched off the port catapult of USS *Salt Lake City* to spot for gunfire during the bombardment and eventual occupation of Kiska, Alaska, by American forces in August 1943. The SOC wears oversize national insignia on the fuselage and national insignia on both sides of the top wing as an additional recognition aid for friendly gunners. The aircraft also carries a white stripe on the vertical stabilize, a theater marking for aircraft operating in waters off the Aleutian Islands. (Real War Photos)

▾ 'White 2,' an SOC-3 from VCS-6, launches off of the starboard side catapult of USS *Minneapolis* for submarine patrol, as the cruiser prepares to raid Wake Island on 5 October 1943. The SOC is armed with a pair of 250-pound bombs, and the gunner has his .30-caliber machine gun in the 'alert' position ready to engage any marauding Japanese aircraft. (Real War Photos)

▲ This SOC has just cleared the port side catapult of the light cruiser USS *Brooklyn* (CL-40) after launching during simulated battle exercises on 12 June 1944. The aircraft is being flown without an observer/gunner, indicating the exercise is being undertaken in friendly waters. The SOC was assigned to Cruiser Scouting Squadron Eight (VCS-8) while the cruiser was operating in the Mediterranean in preparation for the invasion of southern France in August 1944. (Real War Photos)

▼ SOC-3 'Black 9,' from VCS-8, is recovered aboard *Brooklyn* while she trains in the Mediterranean on 18 June 1944, off the North West Africa Area of Operations in preparation for the invasion of southern France. The aircraft will be turned 180 degrees to be placed on the catapult and readied for the next flight. (Real War Photos)

▼ An SOC-3 from VCS-6 is hooked to the recovery cable of USS *Minneapolis* after spotting for main battery fire during a raid on on Kwajalein in the Marshall Islands in January 1944. The Seagull will soon be placed on the port catapult of the heavy cruiser, and the pilot will keep the engine running until he nears the catapult. (Real War Photos)

▲ An Aviation Machinists Mate (AAM) sits on an SOC-3 of Cruiser Scouting Squadron Twelve (VCS-12) to have his picture taken as the aircraft rests on the catapult of the light cruiser USS *Montpelier* (CL-57) at her home base of Subic Bay, Philippines, in April 1945. The hook that engages the landing net is clearly visible on the main float. (Real War Photos)

Recovery Sled

The recovery sled, sometimes referred to as a 'plane trap' or 'sea sled,' was a landing and recovery aid towed by a line from a boom over the side of the ship. It was constructed of heavy-grade canvas and cargo netting so as to present a smooth surface. Red flags at the leading corners served as visual indicators for the pilot. The floatplane taxied onto the sled and then drifted backwards until a hook on the underside of the float engaged the netting. The pilot then cut the engine, and the radioman climbed atop the fuselage to attach the ship's recovery crane hook to the aircraft. Using this technique, floatplanes could be be recovered while the ship was underway.

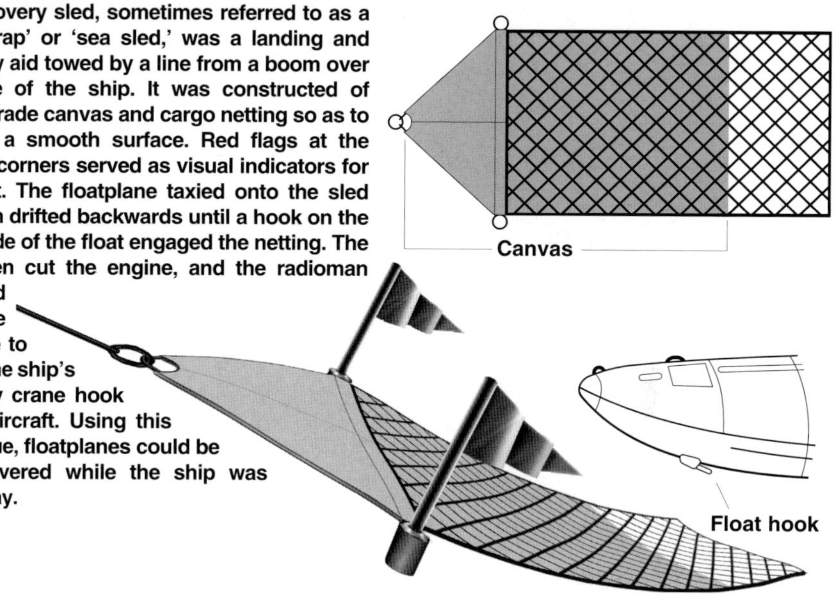

◄ A pair of SOC-3s (BuNos 1126 and 1127) from Marine Scouting Squadron Two (VMS-2) sits on the ramp at San Diego, California, in 1939. A parachute harness hangs from the right wing strut of 1127, ready for action. The cowl and fuselage stripe are Red, and the rudder is painted, from front to back, in Blue, White, and Red. Both these aircraft were converted to SOC-3A standards and were lost at sea while operating with VS-201 off the escort carrier USS *Long Island* (AVG-1). Marine Scouting Squadron Three-M (VMS-3M) also operated twelve SOC-3s. (The Tailhook Association)

An SOC-3A (BuNo 9856) from the Utility unit of USS *Wasp* (CV-7) takes off from the deck of the new fleet carrier in 1940. The aircraft is painted overall aluminum with Orange Yellow top wing upper surfaces. The Neutrality Patrol star is painted on the forward fuselage just ahead of the floatation gear. Two venturi tubes are placed on cabane struts for instruments requiring suction. This aircraft had been converted from an an SOC-1 to SOC-3A standards. (The Tailhook Association)

The U.S. Coast Guard (USCG) received the last three SOC-3s built (BuNos 1144–1146) in 1938, designating them SOC-4 and assigning them serial numbers V171–V173 respectively. The aircraft is painted overall aluminum with Orange Yellow upper wing surfaces. The upper third of the rudder is Insignia Blue, and the vertical stripes below are Insignia Red and insignia White. The USCG emblem is placed low on the forward fuselage. (U.S. Coast Guard)

V172, the USCG's second SOC-4, sits on a rollaround trolley as the crew familiarizes itself with the layout of the cockpit and instruments. The letters 'USCG' are painted on the lower right wing, and the serial number is repeated on the lower left wing. In 1942, V172 was transferred to the U.S. Navy, converted to SOC-3A standards, and assigned BuNo 48244. (U.S. Coast Guard)

▲ This SON-1 has touched down and is taxiing up to engage the streamed out recovery sled of USS *Memphis* (CL-13). The aircraft is covered with salt spray as it approaches the side of the ship. (Real War Photo)

▶ A SON-1 from Cruiser Scouting Squadron Two (VCS-2) makes a high angle approach to land on the slick made when *Memphis* made a turn to starboard. The flaps and leading edge slats are deployed, enabling the floatplane to touch down at 65 mph. (Real War Photos)

▼ The SON-1 is about to engage the recovery sled, using the red flags on either side as a guide. The aircraft is still armed with hundred-pound bombs on each wing and is probably returning from a submarine-scouting mission. The observer will soon climb out of the rear cockpit to catch an awaiting cable and attach it to the wing top to complete the recovery process. (Real War Photos)

▲ The SON-1 now has the recovery cable attached and is being swung aboard to be situated on the starboard catapult, as the recovery crew, with fending-off poles at the ready, waits to bring the floatplane aboard. All of the crew assigned to recover the plane are wearing life jackets in the event they are knocked overboard during the recovery. (Real War Photos)

▲ Safely aboard, and with the engine shut down, this SON-1 sits on the port catapult of USS *Memphis*. The pilot has shut down the engine. The aircraft will soon be drained of fuel, the ordnance department will remove the bombs, and the aircraft will be serviced and checked for any defects noted by the pilot or observer/gunner/radioman. (Real War Photos)

▼ 'Black 6,' an SON-1 from VCS-7, departs into the wind off the starboard catapult of the heavy cruiser USS *Tuscaloosa* operating in the Atlantic on 19 July 1943. The practice bomblet dispenser mounted on the left wing indicates this is a training flight. (Real War Photos)

OS2U Kingfisher

During 1937, the U.S. Navy asked all interested aircraft manufacturers to submit a single aircraft for evaluation to replace the Vought O3U-6 floatplane, calling for a two-seat observation aircraft small enough to operate, without folding wings, from a battleship, and which also could be easily converted to a landplane.

Three companies submitted aircraft to meet the specifications. Stearman's entry was their Model 85, a tandem two-seat biplane of mixed metal and fabric construction, designated XOSS-1. The Naval Aircraft Factory also submitted a biplane design of mixed construction, the XOSN-1. The final entry was the Vought-Sikorsky Model VS-310, a mid-wing monoplane designated XOS2U-1 (BuNo 0951), which made its first flight as a landplane on 1 March 1938, a full three months ahead of the other two entries. The Vought prototype, when configured as a floatplane, became the first monoplane to be catapulted from a ship.

The XOS2U-1 was also of mixed construction, employing an all-aluminum monocoque fuselage with the forward portion of the wings constructed of spot-welded sheet steel and the rear portion fabric-covered. The wing featured 'drooping' ailerons, which lowered with the flaps to create, in effect, full-span flaps that reduced landing speed while increasing lateral control. Spoilers on top of the wing provided roll control when the flaps were lowered. Wingspan was 35 feet 11 inches (10.95 m), and length was 33 feet 7 inches (10.24 m). The XOS2U-1 weighed 3,213 pounds (1,457.4 kg) and had a maximum speed of 170 miles per hour (273.6 km/hr) as a floatplane.

The Navy tested all three entries, announced that Vought was the winner, and placed an order for fifty-four production aircraft designated OS2U-1 (BuNos 1681–1734).

The OS2U-1 differed from the prototype in the shape of the observer's canopy and an enlarged support for its EDO float, which replaced the original Vought-designed float. The engine was upgraded from the Pratt & Whitney R-985-4 to the 450-horsepower R-985-48 Wasp nine-cylinder radial air-cooled engine, and extended exhaust pipes replaced the flush exhaust pipes of the XOS2U-1. The OS2U-1 was armed with a single fixed .30-caliber machine gun with six hundred rounds for the pilot and a flexible .30-caliber machine gun, also with six hundred rounds, for the observer/radio operator. Underwing weapons racks could be fitted to carry hundred-pound or 250-pound bombs or 325-pound depth charges.

The OS2U-1 had a maximum speed of 175 mph (281.6 km/hr), a service ceiling of 19,000 feet (5,791.2 m), and a maximum range of 982 miles (1580 km). Empty weight was 4,123 pounds (1,870 kg), and maximum weight was 5,600 pounds (2540 kg). Of the fifty-four built, forty-nine were built with EDO floats, and five were constructed as landplanes and assigned to land bases. The floatplanes were initially assigned to Battleship Observation Squadrons (VO).

The first production OS2U-1 (BuNo 1681) was bailed (loaned) to Northrop Aircraft to test a new type of wing flap (known as the 'Zap flap' for its designer, Ed Zap), intended to be installed on Northrop's P-61 Black Widow.

While OS2U-1 production was proceeding, the Navy on 4 December 1939 issued an order for 158 improved versions of the Kingfisher, designated OS2U-2 (BuNos 2189–2288 and 3073–3130). The improvements consisted of self-sealing fuel tanks, 140 pounds of armor for the crew, and additional fuel tanks in the inner wing panels increasing fuel capacity to 240 gallons, 96 gallons over the earlier OS2U-1. The fuel system was also fitted with a carbon dioxide gas purge system to prevent buildup of explosive vapors. With these improvements, the maximum weight rose to 6,108 pounds, causing a loss of 7 mph in maximum speed.

The contract called for the construction of forty-five OS2U-2 as seaplanes and the balance as landplanes. EDO also supplied an additional seventy sets of floats so the landplanes could be converted to floatplanes. The majority of the landplanes were delivered to Naval Air (▸▸ 22)

▾ The prototype Vought XOS2U-1 (BuNo 0951) made its first fight on 1 March 1938 as a landplane, powered by a Pratt & Whitney R-985-4 air-cooled radial engine. The fuselage was constructed of aluminum, while the wings were of mixed construction of welded sheet steel and fabric. All moveable flying surfaces were fabric-covered. (LTV)

▾ The single XOS2U-1 made its first flight as a floatplane on 19 May 1938, taking off from Long Island Sound and piloted by Vought test pilot Paul S. Baker. The aircraft was painted overall in dark blue with the rudder, forward edge of the cowl, and the cowl flaps painted silver. The EDO main and wingtip floats were natural metal. (LTV)

Stations (NAS) Jacksonville and Pensacola, Florida, to be used in the formation of Inshore Patrol Squadrons for coastal antisubmarine reconnaissance and convoy escort duties. The Navy eventually formed thirty Inshore Patrol Squadrons along the east and west coasts of the United States and the Gulf of Mexico, as well as in Cuba, Panama, and Hawaii. The OS2U-2 also was used in the training role at NAS Jacksonville, NAS Pensacola, and NAS Corpus Christi, Texas.

The final production model of the Kingfisher, the OS2U-3, would also be the most widely produced version, with some 1,006 constructed. On 23 May 1941 the Navy issued contract Number C76493 for the construction of 970 OS2U-3s (BuNos 5284–5941, 6973–5989, and 09393–09692) powered by the Pratt & Whitney R-984-AN-2, an engine common to both the Army and Navy. Vought also produced additional OS2U-3 ship-sets for use as repair parts aboard ship, and some of these sets were built up into complete aircraft with no BuNo assigned.

In order to allow Vought to concentrate on the production of the F4U Corsair, the NAF produced a further three hundred OS2U-3s during 1942 as OS2N-1s (BuNos 01216–01515), and following the close of its Kingfisher production, Vought turned over to the NAF enough ship-sets of parts to construct another thirty-one aircraft (BuNos 6942–6972).

A few OS2N-1s were assigned to destroyer operations in the Pacific. Six *Fletcher* class destroyers were modified to carry one OS2U/OS2N floatplane by replacing the number three 5-inch mount with a catapult.

The final version of the Kingfisher, the XOS2U-4, was an experimental version of the OS2U-2. Two OS2U-2s (BuNos 2189 and 3975) were fitted with 'Zap flap' wings, similar to those fitted to Northrop's OS2U-1 (BuNo 1681), but with the ability to fold as in Grumman's TBF Avenger and F4F Wildcat. The intention was to install the Zap flap on future Kingfishers, but the Navy opted to discontinue OS2U production in favor of the single seat Curtiss SC-1.

The Kingfisher was the most widely produced floatplane during World War II. In addition to the U.S. Navy, it served with the Royal Navy, the Royal Australian Air Force, Chile, the Netherlands, Uruguay, and Argentina. (▸▸ 39)

▲ **The XOS2U-1 sits on a dolly used to move the floatplane while it is on land. The aircraft is now painted aluminum overall with Orange Yellow upper wing surfaces. Early tests indicated a need for more stability at the rear of the float, and a third strut was added to correct the problem. The prototype remained active as a test aircraft until May 1944. (LTV)**

▼ **An OS2U-2 (BuNo 2278) assigned to the battleship USS *North Carolina* (BB-55) sits on a Vought float and beaching gear in 1940, prior to its assignment to the new Battleship Observation Squadron (VO-6). The aircraft is camouflaged in the overall nonspecular Light Gray scheme introduced in 1940. The ship's name is painted in white on the lower aft fuselage. (LTV)**

Three OS2U-1s from Scouting Squadron 1, 1st Naval District (VS1D1), Squantum, Massachusetts, fly in formation over the Atlantic in 1942. The aircraft are painted in nonspecular Blue Gray over nonspecular Light Gray with nonspecular Insignia Red and Insignia White stripes on the rudder. All are armed with hundred-pound bombs. (LTV)

An OS2U-2 (BuNo 2190) from Inshore Patrol Squadron 6, in the Fourth Naval District (VS-4-D1), Cape May, New Jersey. Inshore Patrol Squadrons were formed to patrol close to the coastline for U-boats and other raiders. The aircraft is finished in overall aluminum with a Red fuselage stripe and cowling and Orange Yellow upper wing surfaces. (LTV)

With the advent of the Neutrality Patrol, the U.S. national insignia was painted on the forward fuselage sides of Navy aircraft as an identification guide to friendly gunners. This OS2U-2 (BuNo 2193) was stationed at Quonset Point, Rhode Island, with VS-2D-1. The cowling and fuselage stripe are Red on an overall aluminum dope finish. (Naval Historical Center)

Vought OS2U/OS2N

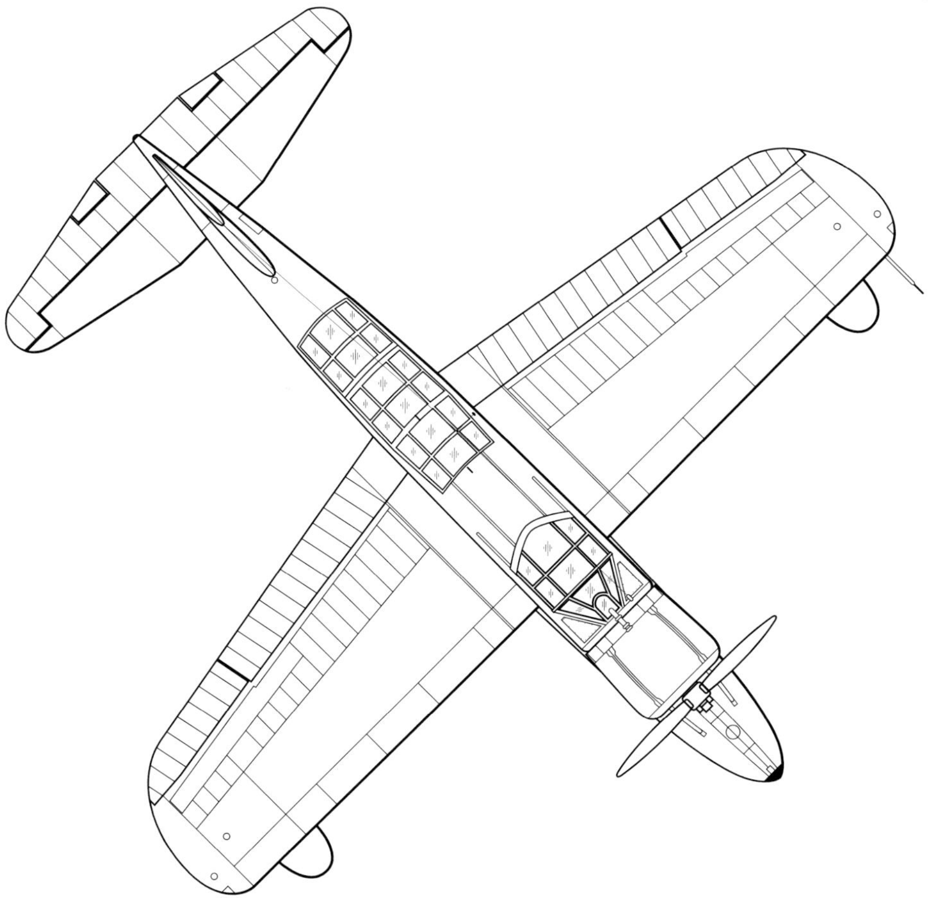

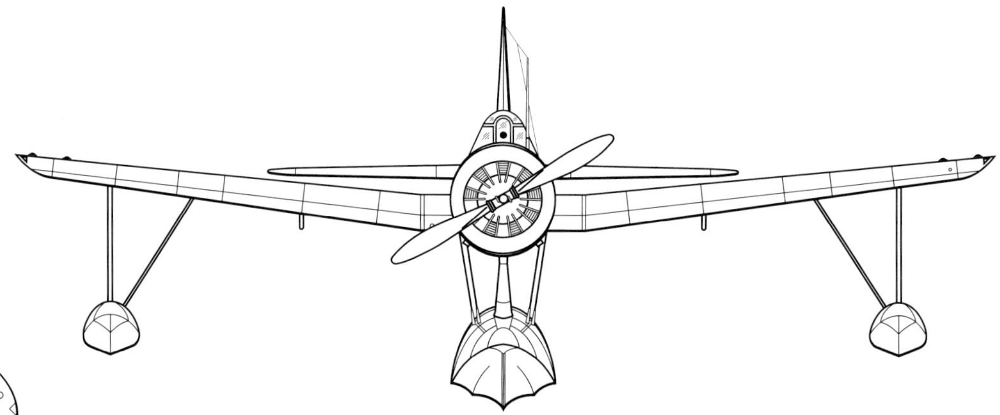

Specifications (OS2U-3)

Length	33 ft 7 in (10.24 m)
Wingspan	35 ft 11 in (10.95 m)
Height	15 ft 1 in (4.59 m)
Weight, empty	4,310 lb (1,955 kg)
Weight, maximum	6,108 lb (2,771 kg)
Engine	One 450 hp Pratt & Whitney R-985-AN-2 Wasp Junior aircooled 9-cylinder radial engine
Armament	One fixed forward-firing .30-caliber (7.62 mm) machine gun One aft-firing .30-caliber (7.62 mm) machine gun on flexible mount
Maximum speed	175 mph (281.6 km/h)
Cruising speed	119 mph (192 km/hr) at 5,000 ft (1,524 m)
Fuel	240 gal (908.5 l)
Range	908 mi (1,461 km)
Rate of climb	416 ft/min (2.1 m/sec)
Service ceiling	19,000 ft (5,791 m)
Crew	2

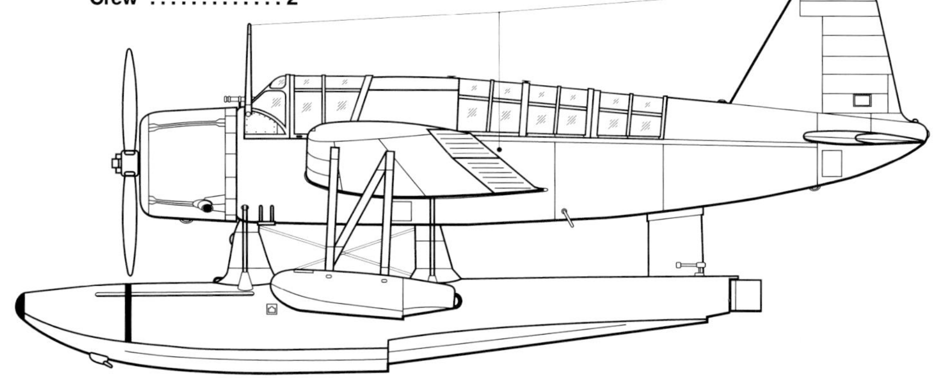

Emblem of VO-1

Curtiss SOC-3 (BuNo 1077), aircraft number '9,' Battleship Observation Squadron One (VO-1), USS *Pennsylvania* (BB-38), fleet flagship for the Battleship Battle Force, San Pedro, California, 1939. Aircraft is overall aluminum with Orange Yellow upper wing top surface. Lower half of cowling is Blue. Unit emblem is carried on forward fuselage.

Curtiss SOC-3, aircraft number '7,' Cruiser Scouting Squadron Seven (VCS-7), heavy cruiser USS *Tuscaloosa* (CA-37), Atlantic Ocean, early 1942. Camouflage is nonspecular Blue-Gray over nonspecular Light Gray.

Curtiss SOC-3, Cruiser Scouting Squadron Five (VCS-5), heavy cruiser USS *Salt Lake City* (CA-25), during the bombardment of Kiska, Alaska, 2 August 1943. Aircraft is camouflaged in the three-color scheme of semigloss Sea Blue, nonspecular Intermediate Blue, and nonspecular Insignia White, with a white stripe on the vertical stabilizer and stars and bars atop both wings.

Vought OS2U-2 Kingfisher (BuNo 2288), Battleship Observation Squadron Six (VO-6), USS *North Carolina* (BB-55), 1940. Paint is overall nonspecular Gray with "NORTH CAROLINA" in white on the fuselage. The aircraft is fitted with a Vought float.

Vought OS2U-3 (BuNo 5468), 'Black 17,' assigned to Naval District Inshore Patrol Squadron VS-1D5 (VS-37), Naval Air Station Norfolk, Virginia, 1942. Aircraft is camouflaged in nonspecular Blue Gray over nonspecular Light Gray with Insignia Red and Insignia White rudder stripes.

▸ Naval Aircraft Factory OS2N-1, 'White 2,' of Cruiser Scouting Squadron Seventeen (VCS-17) aboard light cruiser U.S.S. *Pasadena* (CL-65) in the West Central Pacific during 1945. Camouflage is semigloss Sea Blue, nonspecular Intermediate Blue, and nonspecular Insignia White, with a nonspecular Insignia White rudder.

◂ Vought OS2U-3, aircraft number '3' of Scouting Observation Utility Squadron Two (SOSU-2) during 1944. Camouflage is semigloss Sea Blue, nonspecular Intermediate Blue, and nonspecular Insignia White, with '3V7' painted on the cowling in small white characters. Exhaust flame dampers were fitted for night operations.

▸ A Curtiss SO3C-1 serving with Cruiser Scouting Squadron Twelve (VCS-12) aboard the light cruiser USS *Denver* (CL-58) during sea trials in the Atlantic on 31 December 1942. Aircraft is camouflaged in nonspecular Blue Gray over nonspecular Light Gray. Yagi radar antennas have been fitted under the wings.

◂ Marking detail ▾

◂ 'WAR JUNK,' a Curtiss SO3C-1 (Bu No unknown) from Cruiser Scouting Squadron Thirteen (VCS-13) serving aboard USS *Biloxi* (CL-80) during the light cruiser's shakedown in the Atlantic in August 1943. Camouflage is semigloss Sea Blue, nonspecular Intermediate Blue, and non-specular Insignia White. The national insignia had an Insignia Red border during that period.

▸ Curtiss SC-1 Seahawk (BuNo 35785), 'White 2,' of Battleship Observation Squadron One B (VO-1B) aboard USS *Iowa* (BB-61) in the Pacific in May 1947. Aircraft is painted overall gloss Sea Blue with float undersurfaces painted nonspecular Insignia White.

▲ 'Black 30,' an OS2U-2 (BuNo 2228) from NAS Pensacola, taxis out into Pensacola Bay for a training mission in 1942. This particular aircraft was used to teach naval aviators in intermediate and advanced flying skills before they were sent to frontline squadrons. The Kingfisher is finished in overall aluminum dope with Orange Yellow wing tops. All markings are Black. (National Archives)

▲ An OS2U-2 is prepared for launch from the battleship USS *Washington* (BB-56) in waters off Great Britain in 1942. Aircraft '9' is camouflaged in nonspecular Blue Gray over nonspecular Light Gray. The cowling front is covered to help keep the engine warm. A ladder has been placed on the port side of the aircraft to assist the flight crew in boarding. (National Archives)

◀ The first OS2U-3 (BuNo 5284), camouflaged in the then-standard scheme of overall nonspecular Light Gray. The propeller is Black with Insignia Red, Orange Yellow, and Insignia Blue warning stripes, and the float has an Insignia Red propeller warning stripe painted on it. The beaching gear was removed before flight once the aircraft was in the water. (LTV)

The pilot's Instrument panel contained a compass, clock, turn and bank indicator, tachometer, oil temperature gauge, rate-of-climb indicator, airspeed indicator, artificial horizon, and altimeter. The fixed .30-caliber machine gun was mounted on the right side of the cockpit, and an ammunition canister containing six hundred rounds was located between the rudder pedals. (National Archives)

An OS2U-3 from VCS-10 is catapulted off the heavy cruiser USS *Boston* (CA-69) in 1943. The OS2U began replacing the Curtiss SOC and SO3C on cruisers in 1943, even though it did not have folding wings. This Kingfisher is camouflaged in the three-color scheme adopted in 1943. The propeller-warning stripe on the float has been painted in a wavy shape. (Real War Photos)

The beaching gear is in place on the float as this OS2U-3 from Scouting Observation Utility Squadron Two (SOSU-2) is prepared for recovery to land. The cowl marking, '2V7,' indicates this is the number two test aircraft operated by the squadron. The aircraft is camouflaged in the three-color scheme adopted in 1943. SOSU-2 operated in the night flying role. (EDO)

Cruiser Catapult

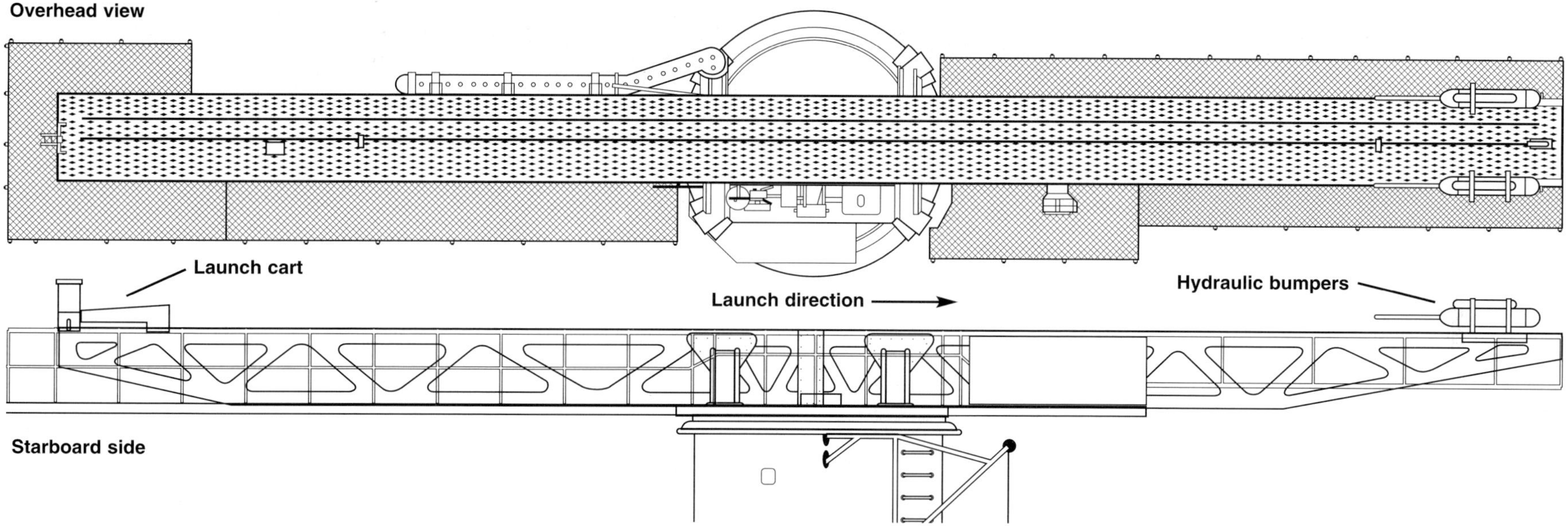

▾ An OS2U-3 is launched off the starboard catapult of the battleship USS *Alabama* (BB-60) in 1943. Another OS2U-3, with the engine running, is positioned on the port catapult and will soon be launched cross-deck into the wind. The third Kingfisher is on a dolly waiting in reserve. All of the 20 mm guns are manned, indicating the ship is operating in a war zone. (EDO)

▼ An ordnance crew prepares to fit 'Black 18,' an OS2U-3 (BuNo 9475) of Naval District NAS Norfolk, Virginia, with hundred-pound bombs for a mission over the Atlantic, using a torpedo dolly to maneuver the ordnance. The OS2U-3 is camouflaged in nonspecular Blue Gray over nonspecular Light Gray. Wartime censors, in the interest of national security, have erased the bomb racks from under the wing. (United Technologies)

▲ Aircraft captains run up the engines of three OS2U-3s of Naval District NAS Norfolk, Virginia, while awaiting the arrival of the aircrew. Each crewman wears a seat pack parachute that doubles as a seat cushion. All aircraft are camouflaged in nonspecular Blue-Gray over nonspecular Light Gray with nonspecular Insignia Red and nonspecular Insignia White stripes on the rudder. (National Archives)

▼ 'Black 17,' an OS2U-3 of Inshore Patrol Squadron VS-2D5, taxies out to the takeoff area in Chesapeake Bay off NAS Norfolk, Virginia, in 1942, and the pilot will soon deploy the full-width flaps for takeoff. The aircraft is armed with a pair of hundred-pound bombs. In this configuration, the Kingfisher had a range of some six hundred miles. (United Technologies)

▲ OS2U-3 'Black 13' (BuNo 5865) of Inshore Patrol Squadron VS-1D5 flies over the Atlantic Ocean on a patrol out of NAS Norfolk, Virginia, in 1942. The observer's .30-caliber machine gun is in the stowed position, and hundred-pound bombs are fitted to the wing racks. VS-1D5 became Scouting Squadron Thirty-Seven (VS-37) in 1943. (National Archives)

▼ OS2U-3 'Black 6' is eased down the ramp on its beaching gear by a tractor (out of photo to right) and cable in preparation for flight off water. The crew, in high waders, will remove the beaching gear once the airplane is afloat. The Kingfisher carries a pair of hundred-pound bombs that can be used against U-boats as well as surface craft. (U.S. Navy)

Aircraft Handling Cranes

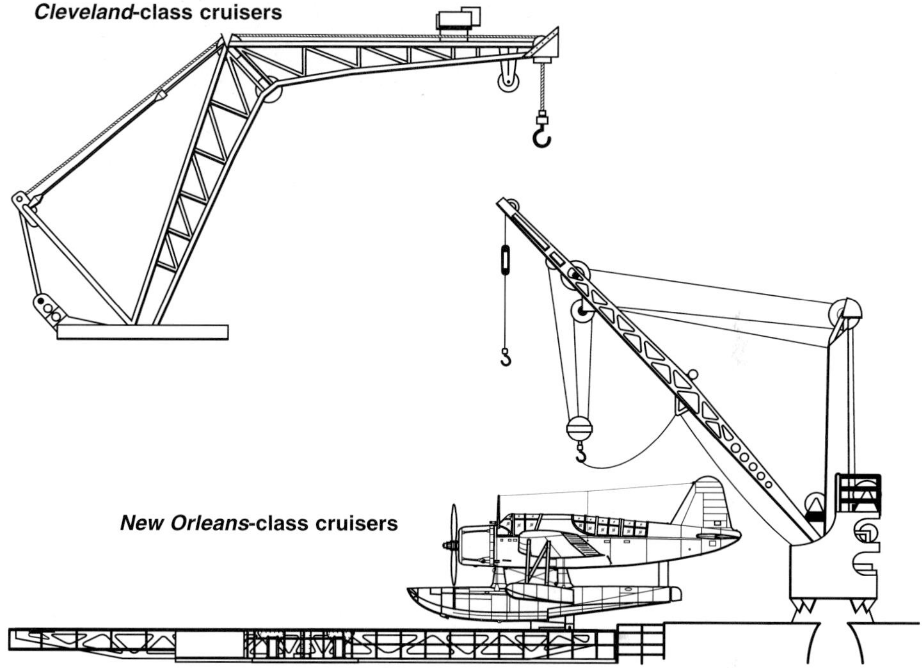

▲ OS2U-3 'Black 71' is washed off following a training mission out of NAS Corpus Christi, Texas, in 1942, as the aircraft's crew chief, with clipboard numbered '71,' awaits his charge. Salt water corrosion was difficult to manage on floatplanes, and constant inspection and cleaning were the norm for aviation machinist's mates. The aircraft is finished in overall aluminum with black lettering. (United Technologies)

▼ Various color schemes abound on these OS2Us at NAS Corpus Christi, Texas, in 1942. Aircraft can be seen in overall yellow, nonspecular Blue Gray with Orange Yellow wing tops, and overall aluminum with Orange Yellow wing tops like the nearest OS2U-3, BuNo 5599. A training session is underway for aircrews. (United Technologies)

▼ The crew of this OS2U-3 from VS-1D3, Naval District New York, deploys a two-man life raft during a training session. Wartime censors have blacked out a portion of the observer's canopy to hide the .30-caliber machine gun. VS-1D3 became Scouting Squadron Thirty-four (VS-34) in 1943. (National Archives)

▲ An OS2U-3 with empty bomb racks is recovered under icy conditions in Woman's Bay, Kodiak, Alaska, in 1943. The tow tug has chains fitted to its wheels to improve traction on the paved ramp. The oversize U.S. national insignia is positioned between the wing float and fuselage. (EDO)

▲ Beach crews of Scouting Squadron Sixty four (VS-64) make an OS2U-3 ready for flight at Halavo seaplane base, Florida, Solomons Island. The machinist mate makes last-minute checks before the Kingfisher's engine is started and warmed up for early morning search patrols in July 1943. (National Archives)

▼ An OS2U-3 about to launched cross-deck from a battleship in late 1942. Her sister aircraft has already been launched, as indicated by the launching sled's position on the catapult. The gunpowder-driven catapult could propel the Kingfisher from 0 to 70 mph, a speed sufficient for flight. (Elsilrac)

▸ An OS2U-3 leaves the catapult on a training flight in waters off Great Britain in 1943. 'Black 9' in camouflaged in nonspecular Blue Gray over nonspecular Light Gray. The U.S. national insignia is applied to the fuselage sides but not to the left lower wing in accordance with a February 1943 directive. The observer is bent forward and holding onto the handholds provided for him. (U.S. Navy)

Observer's Machine Gun

Gun stowed

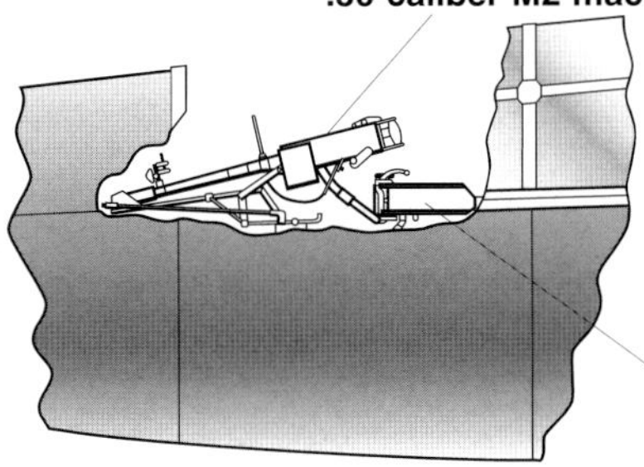

Gun deployed

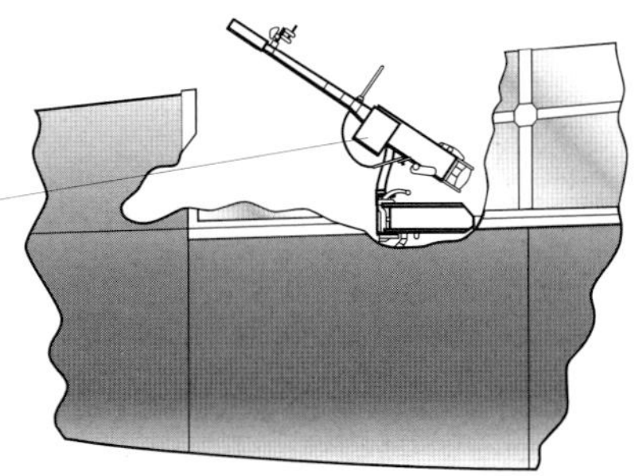

▾ The Kingfisher's observer was provided with a Colt-Browning M-2 .30-caliber machine gun with six hundred rounds of ammunition and sat in a Scarff ring that could rotate 360 degrees. This seat is situated in the forward position, and the gun is in the stowed position. The ammunition canister is fitted to the left side of the breech. The interior of the Kingfisher was painted a dull dark green. (National Archives)

▼ The first rescue at sea by a Kingfisher took place on 23 March 1944, when Lt JG Denver F. Baxter landed his OS2U-3 in the lagoon of Truk Island and rescued Lt JG George M. Blair, an F6F-3 Hellcat pilot from Fighting Squadron Nine (VF-9), who had been shot down by Japanese anti-aircraft fire. The Kingfisher's observer/gunner, Aviation Chief Radioman Rouben F. Hickman, who had thrown his parachute away to make room for Lt Blair, holds the lifting sling tight and awaits the arrival of the hook to hoist the plane aboard the heavy cruiser USS *Baltimore*. The Kingfisher and crew were from Scouting Squadron Ten (VCS-10). (National Archives)

▲ An OS2U-3 from Battleship Observation Squadron Two (VO-2), operating off Fleet Flagship USS *Pennsylvania*, spots for gunfire as elements of the 1st U.S. Marine Division move ashore for the invasion of Angaur, Palau Islands, on 15 September 1944. (LTV)

▼ As an audience watches, an OS2U-3 from Cruiser Scouting Squadron Three (VCS-3), armed with a pair of hundred-pound bombs, is launched from the heavy cruiser USS *Pensacola* (CA-24) in 1944 for a scouting mission in the Pacific. The OS2U began serving following the failure of the Curtiss SO3C-1 to live up to expectations during sea trials. (Real War Photos)

An OS2U-3 of Scouting Observation Service Unit Three (SOSU-3), an advanced operational training unit, sits on the flight line at NAS Alameda, California, in January 1946. The Kingfisher is painted in the three-color scheme adopted in 1943. No national insignia is painted on the lower left wing, in accordance with standard practice at the time. The OS2U will soon be sent to the scrappers for disposal. (Fred C. Dickey Jr.)

A flagman displays a green flag to indicate that the OS2U-3 can be hoisted aboard USS *South Dakota* (BB-57) on 29 April 1943 during operations in the Pacific. The Kingfisher's antenna has been lowered, and the cable containing the hook is being positioned so the observer can attach it to the aircraft. The Kingfisher was assigned to Battleship Observation Squadron Nine (VO-9). (Naval Historical Center)

An OS2U-3 armed with hundred-pound bombs is hoisted aboard an unidentified cruiser operating in the Pacific. The observer stands next to the pilot as the catapult officer, who is holding onto a covered 20 mm Oerlikon cannon, signals to the crane operator to position the Kingfisher. In the background is the aircraft carrier USS *Yorktown* (CV-10). (National Archives)

Floats/Landing Gear

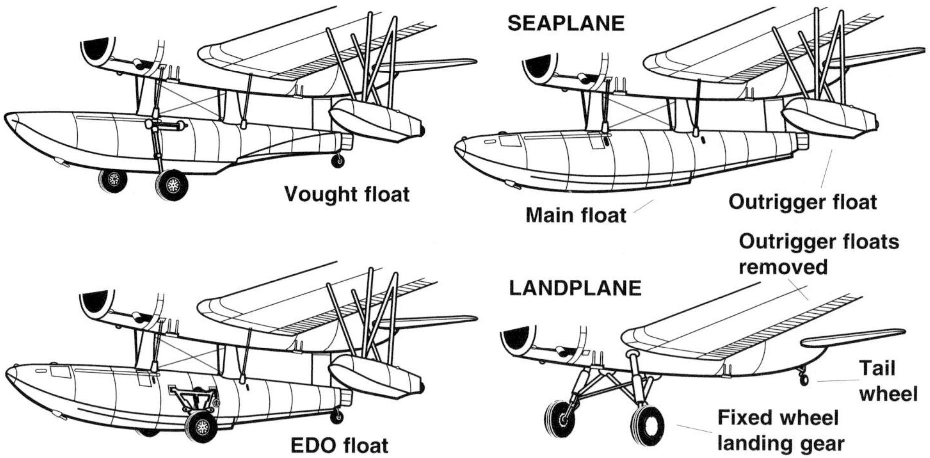

▲ 'White W6,' an OS2U-3 from SOSU-3, sits on its beaching gear at NAS Alameda, California, in January 1946. The Kingfisher is painted gloss Sea Blue over gloss White. In the background are a few Curtiss SC-1 Seahawks, the floatplanes that would eventually replace Kingfishers aboard ship. (Fred C. Dickey Jr.)

▼ A factory fresh OS2N-1 (BuNo 01254) sits on beaching gear just outside the Naval Aircraft Factory (NAF) in 1942. The NAF officially produced three hundred OS2U–3s in 1942, and Vought turned over enough ship sets for the NAF to construct another thirty-one. The OS2N-1 is camouflaged in nonspecular Blue Gray over nonspecular Light Gray with nonspecular Insignia Red and nonspecular Insignia White rudder stripes. (National Archives)

A OS2N-1 flies out over the Atlantic on a training flight in 1942. The pilot has no telescopic sight, and the observer/gunner has no machine gun. The Kingfisher is camouflaged in nonspecular Blue Gray over nonspecular Light Gray. The cowl flaps are open to help regulate the temperature of the R-985 radial engine. (National Archives)

An OS2N-1 from Scouting Squadron Sixty-four (VS-64) gets a sixty-hour check at Halavo Seaplane Base, Solomon Islands, in late 1943. The oil will be changed, the propeller adjusted, the engine checked for leaks, and the airframe checked for corrosion. The squadron artist is applying the squadron's emblem (a turtle holding a telescope). (National Archives)

A hundred-pound bomb is positioned by ordnance crew on a OS2N-1 aboard a *Fletcher*-class destroyer operating in the Pacific in 1943. The OS2N-1 sits on the catapult that replaced the destroyer's number three 5-inch mount. The U.S. national insignia has been painted between the float struts and the bomb shackle. (National Archives)

Curtiss SO3C Seamew

In 1938 the U.S. Navy entertained proposals for a new floatplane to replace the Curtiss SOC. Specifications called for a wingspan no greater than 38 feet (11.57 m) and a folded span no greater than 15 feet (4.57 m), so as to enable the aircraft to fit in the hangar bays of cruisers. Maximum allowable weight was 6,350 pounds (2,880.3 kg), and maximum landing speed was 55 mph (88.5 km/hr). The aircraft was to be powered by a Ranger XV-770-4 inverted inline V-12 air-cooled engine, a new and experimental powerplant. Curtiss entered the XSO3C, and Vought the XSO2U-1.

The winning XSO3C-1 (BuNo 1385) was a mid-wing monoplane with a central EDO float and outer wing stabilizing floats. Its wingspan was 38 feet, and overall length was 37 feet (11.28 m). Height, including the float, was 15 feet 3 inches (4.65 m). The wings folded much like those of the Grumman TBF and F4F. Empty weight was 4,250 pounds (1,928 kg), and maximum takeoff weight was 5,860 pounds (2,658 kg). The Ranger engine produced six hundred horsepower for takeoff and four hundred horsepower at 9,000 feet (2,743 m). Maximum range was 930 miles (1,497 km) on internal fuel of 126 gallons (476.96 l).

The XSO3C also could be equipped with landing gear for operations as a landplane, and the prototype made its first flight on conventional landing gear. It also had a ventral fin to increase directional stability when floats were installed, but this was eliminated from production models.

The production model SO3C-1 also differed in several other respects. Both the fuselage fuel tank and armored pilot's seat were removed in order to save weight, and upturned tips were added to the wing to improve aerodynamic efficiency. Cowlings were modified in an attempt to improve engine cooling, a problem that was to plague the SO3C during its service life. The pilot's canopy was given a more rounded shape, and an extended dorsal fin was added to the observer's canopy. A single fixed .30-caliber (7.7 mm) machine gun was fitted for the pilot, and a single .30-caliber machine gun on a flexible mount was provided for the observer/radio operator.

A total of 141 SO3C-1s were produced (BuNos 4730–4783 and 4793–4879). Fifty-six served aboard the new *Cleveland*-class light cruisers and the heavy cruiser USS *Baltimore* (CA-65) beginning in July 1942. However, the SO3C-1 was found to be completely inadequate for its intended role, and by the end of 1943 it had largely been replaced by the older SOC or the newer Vought OS2U.

The SO3C-1B was a proposed version for the Royal Navy but was superseded by the SO3C-2C. A few SO3C-1Cs were converted to target drones, designated SO3C-1K. The next production model was the SO3C-2, with a total of two hundred ordered (BuNos 4880–5029 and 04149–04198). The SO3C-2A was fitted with fixed landing gear and arresting gear for carrier operations and could carry a five hundred-pound bomb on a centerline rack.

The Royal Navy ordered 259 SO3C-2Cs, which featured a Ranger V-770-8 engine, a 24-volt electrical system, and improved radio equipment. In Royal Navy service, the SO3C-2C was named the Seamew 1, a name also adopted by the U.S. Navy. However, the SO3C-2C was also found to be unsuitable, and two hundred of the total order were cancelled.

The last production model of the SO3C was the SO3C-3, a model similar to the SO3C-2, but with reduced weight, a Ranger V-770-8 engine, and no provision for carrier operations. A total of 699 were ordered, but only fifty-nine were built (BuNos 0425–04289).

The SO3C-4 was a proposed version of the SO3C-3, having arresting gear and catapult connection points. A proposed SO3C-4B for the Royal Navy showed no improvement and was rejected. A final version, having a tapered wing without the upturned tips of the SO3C, was proposed by Ryan as the SOR, but no contracts were forthcoming.

A total of 795 of all versions of the SO3C were constructed by Curtiss in their Columbus, Ohio facility. For the most part they were found to be inadequate for military service, in no small measure due to the Navy's mandate to use the Ranger air-cooled inline engine. (▸▸ 45)

▲ The prototype XSO3C-1 (BuNo 1385) seen fitted with beaching gear on 16 February 1940. The aircraft is armed with a pair of bombs under the wings, and an auxiliary ventral fin has been installed under the rear fuselage to increase stability. The engine mandated was the 450-horsepower twelve-cylinder inverted-V air-cooled Ranger XV-770, an untried engine that doomed the SO3C to failure. (National Archives)

▼ By 1942, production SO3C-1s were being flown on training missions prior to their assignments to Navy cruisers. The SO3C-1 differed from the prototype in the shape and size of the vertical stabilizer, the shape of the engine cowling, the elimination of the auxiliary ventral fin, and the installation of upturned wingtips. The SO3C was officially named 'Seamew' in 1942. (U.S. Navy)

▲ The recovery crew on USS *Denver* (CL-58) awaits an SO3C-1 as it approaches the recovery sled streamed out from the ship. The sea state is fairly calm, eliminating any necessity for the ship to make a landing slick, the usual practice in rough seas. (Real War Photos)

▲ The SO3C-1, from Cruiser Scouting Squadron Twelve (VCS-12), taxies up to *Denver*'s recovery sled. The observer will soon attach the recovery cable, and the Seamew will be hoisted onto the waiting catapult. (Real War Photos)

▼ An SO3C-1 (BuNo 4876) of Cruiser Scouting Squadron Twelve (VCS-12) is hooked up by the observer/gunner prior to loading aboard the light cruiser USS *Columbia* (CL-56) in November 1942 for sea trials. This aircraft is painted nonspecular Blue Gray over nonspecular Light Gray, and no propeller spinner is fitted. (Real War Photos)

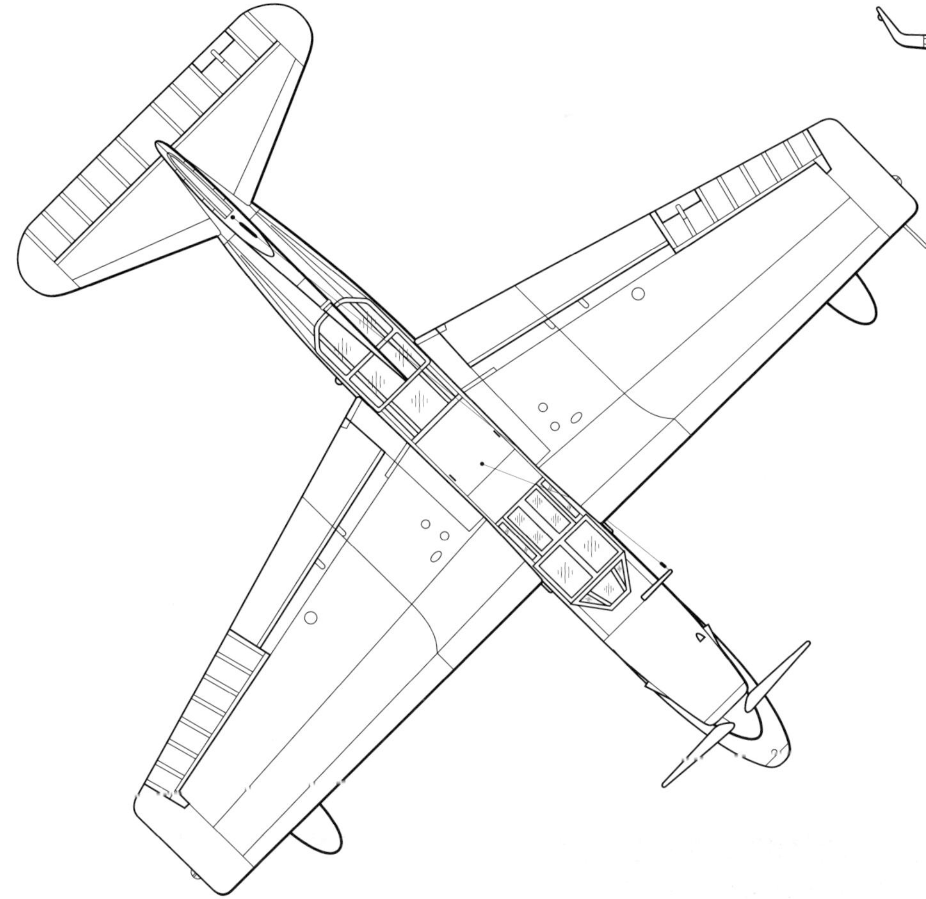

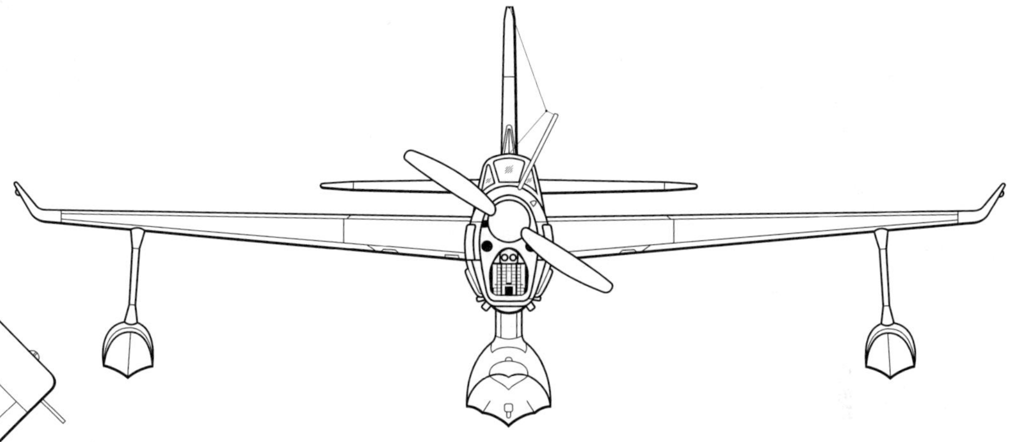

Specifications

Length .... 33 ft 9 in (10.29 m)
Wingspan .... 38 ft (11.58 m)
Height .... 3.45 m
Weight, empty ... 4,995 lb (2,265.7 kg)
Weight, maximum . 7,000 lb (3,175.2 kg)
Engine .... One Ranger V-770-6 550 hp aircooled 12 cylinder inverted-Vee
Armament .... One fixed forward-firing .30-caliber (7.62 mm) machine gun
One aft-firing .30-caliber (7.62 mm) machine gun on flexible mount
Maximum speed .. 167 mph (268.8 km/hr)
Cruising speed ... 125 mph (201 km/hr)
Fuel .... 126 gal (477 l)
Range, maximum . 930 mi (1,497 km)
Rate of climb .... 720 ft/min (3.7 m/sec)
Service ceiling .. 16,500 ft (5,029.2 m)
Crew 2

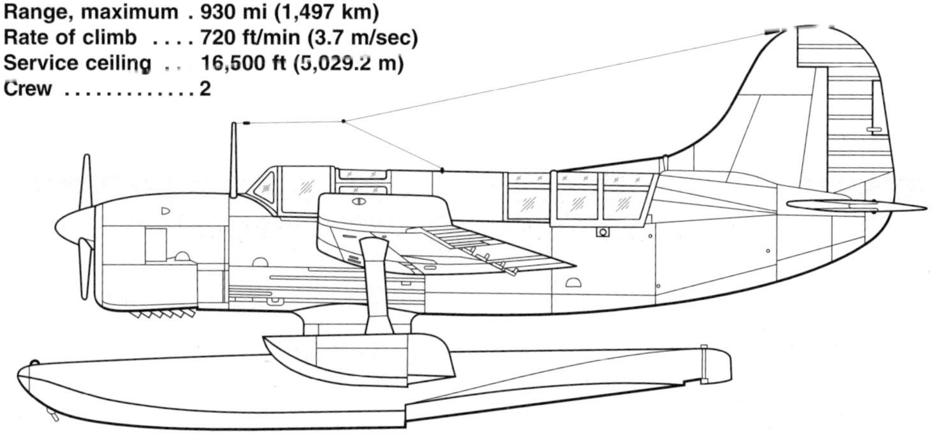

An SO3C-1 approaches the camera plane. The propeller spinner has been removed in an attempt to help cool the engine, and cowl flaps are fully deployed to also aid in engine cooling. The leading edge of the Seamew's vertical stabilizer extended over the observer's canopy to provide extra fin area for directional stability. (Via The Tailhook Association)

In this December 1942 view, an SO3C-1 from Cruiser Scouting Squadron Twelve (VCS-12) is positioned by USS *Denver*'s catapult crew using fending-off poles to help align the Seamew on the catapult. Yagi radar antennas are fitted outboard the wing float. A sister aircraft, seen in the distance just to the right of the left wing float, approaches the ship for recovery following a landing. (Real War Photos)

The folding wing of an SO3C-1 demonstrated at the Curtiss factory in April 1942. The wing hinge point of production aircraft was moved outboard so that the tip floats did not have to be folded when the wing was folded. (National Archives)

▲ A pair of SO3C-1s sits on *Denver*'s fantail catapults during sea trials in December 1942 as recovery sleds are brought aboard. The aircraft handling crane was used to position the aircraft on the catapults and to aid in recovery. The crane was also utilized to bring aboard heavy supplies when the ship was in port. (Real War Photos)

▲ One of two SO3C-1s lost by USS *Denver* on 24 January 1943. According to official reports, BuNo 4804 crashed and sank, and BuNo 4861 crashed at sea five minutes after a catapult launch later that same day. This is probably BuNo 4861, and is the same aircraft shown at lower left. (National Archives)

▼ A crashed SO3C-1 (BuNo 4861?) from VCS-12 is brought aboard *Denver* on 24 January 1943 following a recovery accident. After assessment by the aircraft maintenance department, the aircraft was placed back in the water and destroyed by the ship's gunfire. *Denver*'s captain wrote that the Seamew was totally unsuitable for operations from ships at sea. (Real War Photos)

▼ The SO3C-2A was the carrier-capable landplane version of the Seamew, fitted with a solid rubber tail wheel, an arresting hook, and catapult connection points. This SO3C-2A is on either a training flight or a test flight prior to acceptance, as indicated by the absence of an observer. The aircraft is camouflaged in the 1942 standard scheme of nonspecular Blue Gray over nonspecular Light Gray. (National Archives)

◀ An SO3C-3 (BuNo 04236) flown by a solo pilot in 1944. The exhaust pipes for the Ranger V-770-8 engine can clearly be seen on the underside of the cowling. The number '638' chalked on the cowling is factory-applied and has no connection to the Bureau Number. Bomb racks and Yagi radar antennas are fitted to the wings. The fully spatted main gear reduced drag. (Via The Tailhook Association)

▼ An SO3C-1 (BuNo 4231) launches off the starboard catapult of the light cruiser USS *Biloxi* (CL-80) in September 1943. Following unsuccessful sea trials, *Biloxi*'s three SO3Cs were replaced by a single Vought OS2U-3 Kingfisher from Cruiser Scouting Squadron Thirteen (VCS-13). This Seamew is camouflaged in the three-color scheme, and the national insignia has a red border. (National Archives)

▼ With his canopy open, a pilot flies out over the Atlantic Ocean in 1943 on a training flight in an SO3C-2A, which has a radio direction finder loop antenna located in the observer's position. Two hundred SO3C-2s were built, but only a few of them were converted for carrier operations. (Via The Tailhook Association)

Curtiss SC Seahawk

Noting the success of Japan's Nakajima/Mitsubishi A6M2-N 'Rufe' float seaplane, the U.S. Navy issued a Request for Proposals for a single-seat floatplane to replace the Curtiss SOC Seagull, SO3C Seamew, and Vought OS2U Kingfisher, but having the offensive armament and performance of a fighter and the capability to be converted to landplane configuration. Curtiss's Model 97 was deemed the most desirable, and a contract was issued in March 1943 for five prototypes, designated XSC-1 (BuNo 34095–34096 and 35298–35300). First flight took place on 16 February 1944, and following testing, the U.S. Navy ordered 946 SC-1s.

The SC-1, named Seahawk, was a single-seat, low-wing monoplane with convertible landing gear and powered by a Wright R-1820-62 turbocharged radial engine producing 1,350 horsepower at sea level and 1,300 horsepower at 25,000 feet (7,620 m). Its wingspan was 41 feet (12.5 m), and overall length was 36 feet 4 inches (11.11 m), including the float. Height was 18 feet (5.49 m). Empty weight was 6,320 pounds (2,867 kg), and maximum gross takeoff weight was 8,600 (pounds (3,901 kg). The pilot was protected by 110 pounds (49.89 kg) of armor in the seat back and windshield. The wings were fitted with leading edge slots to improve low-speed performance and could fold flat against the fuselage for ease of storage aboard ship. An AN/APS-4 radar pod could be fitted on the starboard wing rack. Armament comprised a pair of .50-caliber (12.7 mm) machine guns, one per wing. Provisions were also made for the carriage of 325-pound depth charges or 250-pound bombs under the wings.

The first 119 production SC-1s were delivered with an odd-looking fixed landing gear. In this configuration, the SC-1 had a maximum speed of 334 mph (539 km/hr) at 25,000 feet, rivaling the aging Grumman F4F Wildcat. With the EDO float attached, maximum sea level speed was 238 mph (383 km/hr) and 313 mph (503.7 km/hr) at 28,600 feet (8,717 m). With 215 gallons (813.8 l) of onboard fuel, range was 1,090 miles (1,754 km). Economical cruising speed was 125 mph (201 km/hr), and stall speed was 61 mph (98 km). Service ceiling when configured as a landplane was 37,300 feet (11,369 m).

Curtiss's Columbus, Ohio, plant produced a total of 562 SC-1s (BuNos 35301–35623, 35625–35797, and 93302–93367) in addition to the five prototypes; the remaining 384 ordered were cancelled by VJ-Day. The first ships to receive the SC-1 were the new heavy cruisers *Alaska* (CB-1) and *Guam* (CB-2), each of which operated four aircraft from Cruiser Scouting Squadron Sixteen (VCS-16).

One SC-1 (BuNo 35302) was re-engined with a Wright R-1820-76 normally aspirated radial engine producing 1,425 horsepower at sea level. The non-turbocharged engine was more economical on fuel, but aircraft performance suffered at altitude. Other changes included a redesigned engine cowling, a bubble canopy without the framing of the SC-1, strakes from the fuselage to the horizontal stabilizer, and an anti-spin extension on the lower rear fuselage. This aircraft was designated XSC-1A and became the prototype for the SC-2.

Following testing, 250 SC-2s (Curtiss Model 97D), were ordered, but due to the end of the war, only ten (BuNos 119529–119538) were completed; the remainder (BuNos 119539–119778) were cancelled. The SC-2 incorporated a Wright 1820-76 radial engine with a modified cowl; wing racks for rockets, bombs, or rescue cells; and a bubble canopy. Other changes included a rudder with a higher aspect ratio, horn-balanced elevators, an antenna relocated to the rear of the canopy, and provisions for a camera. An AN/ASP-4 radar pod or a 90-gallon (341 l) fuel tank could be fitted to the starboard wing or, when the float was removed, under the centerline of the fuselage. The tenth production model had a jump seat fitted behind the pilot and was designated as a scout-rescue aircraft.

Curtiss Seahawks served until 1949, when Observation Squadron One and Two (VO-1 and 2) gave up their SC-1s and -2s, bringing a colorful era to an end. The catapult-launched floatplane, once essential to the U.S. Navy, would be replaced by helicopters, radar, and other electronic devices.

▾ One of the five XSC-1prototypes on a test flight in 1944. The SC-1s were the only single-seat floatplanes to serve onboard U.S. Navy cruisers and battleships during World War II. The XSC-1 was powered by a 1,350-horsepower Wright Cyclone R-1820-62 nine-cylinder air-cooled radial engine that gave it a top speed of 313 miles per hour. (Via Tailhook Association)

▾ This SC-1 has engaged the recovery sled and will soon be swung aboard the new heavy cruiser USS *Chicago* (CA-136) during sea trials in the Atlantic in March 1945. The Seahawk has an AN/APS-4 radar pod fitted to the right wing and a practice bomb dispenser under the left wing. (Real War Photos)

▲ SC-1 'White 1' has engaged the recovery sled and soon will be swung aboard the heavy cruiser USS *Guam* (CB-2). The pilot has folded down the antenna and is standing in his seat to reach over the windshield to retrieve the lifting cable. The engine is kept running until the recovery cable is engaged and hooked up. (Via The Tailhook Association)

▲ 'White 2,' an SC-1 from Cruiser Division Sixteen (VCS-16), is swung aboard the heavy cruiser USS *Alaska* (CB-1), operating off the Philippines in Leyte Gulf, on 29 June 1945. The SC-1 is camouflaged in the three-color scheme that would soon be replaced by an overall gloss Sea Blue finish. (Real War Photos)

◄ 'White 2,' an SC-1 from Cruiser Scouting Squadron Thirteen (VCS-13), is recovered aboard the starboard side of USS *Birmingham* (CL-62) on 24 January 1945 while the light cruiser sails toward Iwo Jima. Meanwhile, 'White 3' has been spotted on the port catapult and is being given a post-flight inspection by an Aircraft Machinist Mate (AAM). (Real War photos)

Curtiss SC-1

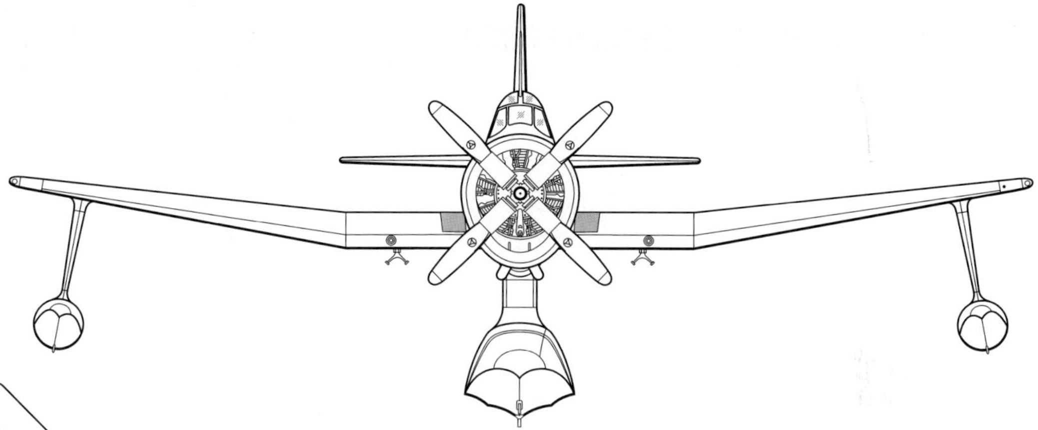

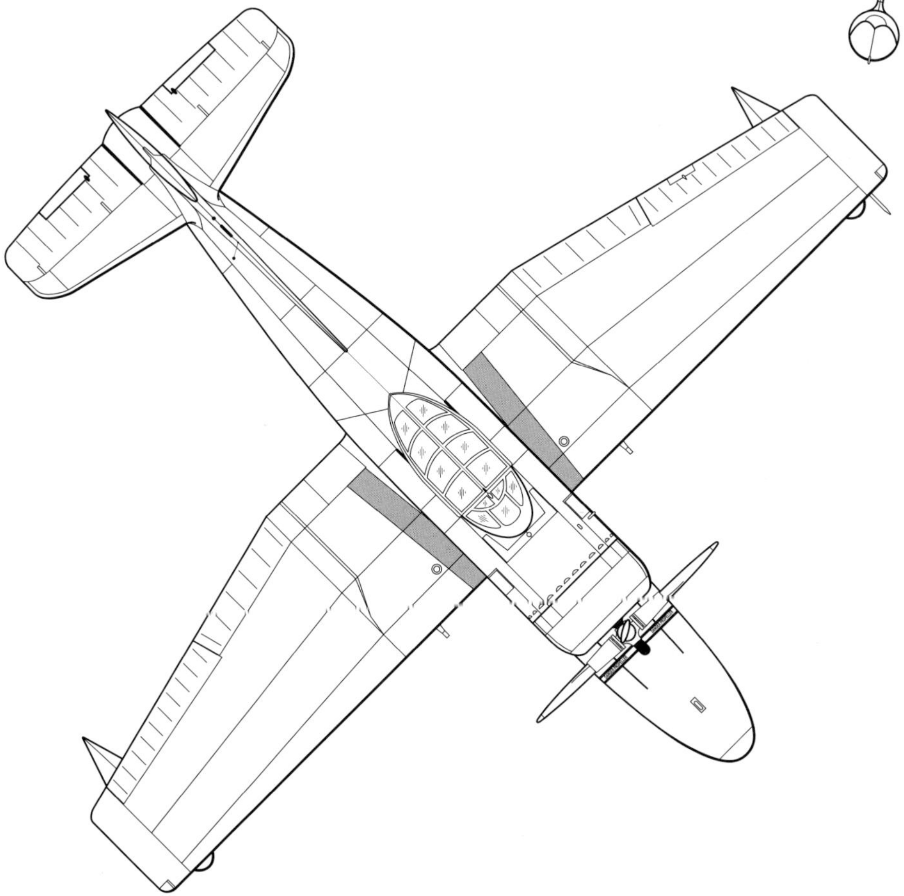

Specifications

Length	36 ft 4½ in (11.09 m)
Wingspan	41 ft (12.5 m)
Height	15 ft 4 in (4.67 m)
Weight, empty	6,320 lb (2,867 kg)
Weight, maximum	7,936 lb (3,600 kg)
Engine	One Wright R-1820-62 'Cyclone' 1,300 hp air-cooled 9-cylinder radial
Armament	Two .50-caliber (12.7 mm) machine guns
Maximum speed	313 mph (503.7 km/hr) at 28,600 ft (8,717 m)
Cruising speed	125 mph (201 km/hr)
Fuel	215 gal (813.8 l)
Range	1,090 mi (1,754 km)
Rate of climb	2,350 ft/min (11.9 m/sec)
Service ceiling	37,300 ft (11,369 m)

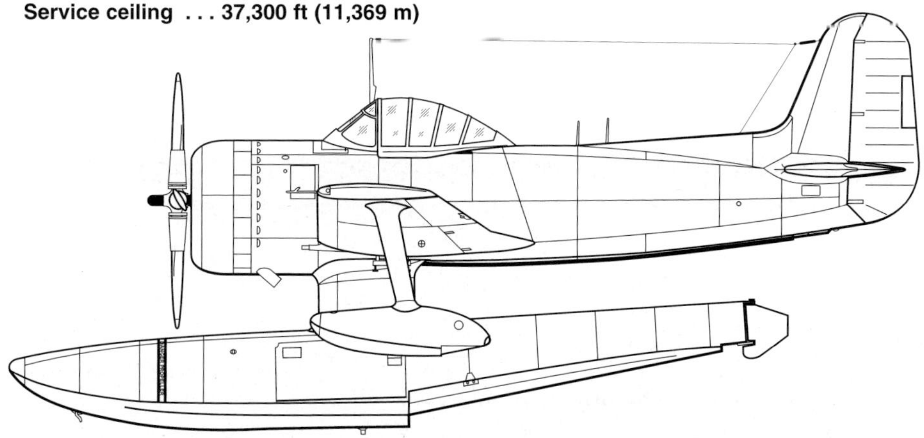

As the ship comes into the wind, 'CF-2,' from Observation Squadron Fifteen-C (VO-15C), is launched off the port catapult of the light cruiser USS *Topeka* (CL-67) in 1947. The SC-1 is finished in the overall gloss Sea Blue scheme adopted in 1944. It has an AN/ASP-4 radar pod under the starboard wing. (Via The Tailhook Association)

XSC-1(BuNo 34096) at Curtiss's Columbus, Ohio, plant on 28 March 1944 with wings extended. The SC-1 is camouflaged in the overall gloss Sea Blue scheme with the undersides of floats painted nonspecular Insignia White. (National Archives)

The same XSC-1 with wings folded. The SC-1's wing fold was similar to that of Grumman's F4F, TBF, and F6F. The muzzle of the port .50-caliber machine gun protrudes from the lower wing. (Via The Tailhook Association)

▲ Various types of beaching gear are lined up awaiting their respective aircraft as 'MC-316,' an SC-1 from Patrol Squadron Five (VPML-5), is brought out of the water at Naval Air Station Jacksonville, Florida, in 1948. The SC-1 was used in the training and 'hack' role until all aircraft of that type were withdrawn in 1949. This SC-1 carries a practice bomblet dispenser on the right wing. (Via Tailhook Association)

▲ A pair of SC-1s from Battleship Observation Squadron One-B (VO-1B) sits on the fantail of the battleship USS *Iowa* (BB-61) in San Francisco Bay, California, 24 May 1947. 'BA-2' (BuNo 35785) is on a trolley with its engine cowling removed for maintenance and inspection. The other SC-1, 'BA-3,' is on the starboard catapult, ready to launch. (Wm. T. Larkins)

▼ One of the ten Curtiss SC-2s built, 'White 4,' (BuNo 119536) sits on the transient aircraft ramp at NAS Pensacola in 1948. The SC-2 differed from the SC-1 in having a full bubble canopy, a relocated antenna mast, a rounded cowling covering the normally aspirated Wright Cyclone R-1820-76 radial, a redesigned lower rear fuselage, and strakes from the fuselage to the horizontal stabilizer. A ninety-gallon extended-range fuel tank is fitted to the centerline rack. (Via Tailhook Association)

Get hooked!

More World War II naval aviation books from Squadron/Signal publications

1081 F2A Buffalo in Action

1097 TBD Devastator in Action

1119 OS2U Kingfisher in Action

1122 SB2U Vindicator in Action

1145 F4U Corsair in Action

1191 F4F Wildcat in Action

5509 F6F Hellcat Walk Around

5533 SBD Dauntless Walk Around

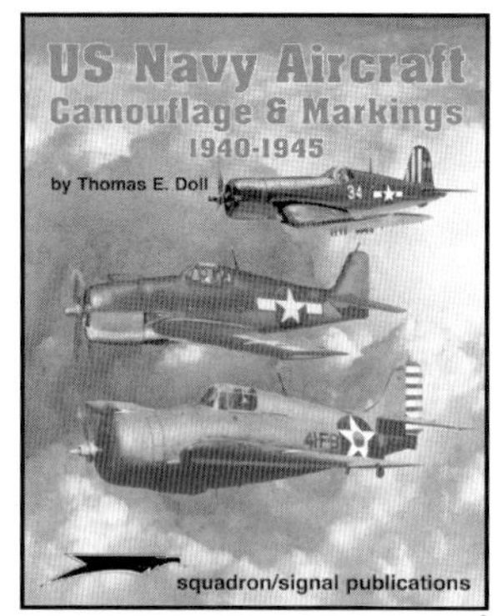

6087
US Navy
Aircraft
Camouflage
&
Markings
1940-1945

For more information on Squadron/Signal books, visit www.squadron.com